THE PUG DOG
ITS HISTORY
AND ORIGINS

by
Wilhelmina Swainston-Goodger

Read Country Books
Home Farm
44 Evesham Road
Cookhill, Alcester
Warwickshire
B49 5lJ

www.readcountrybooks.com

ISBN No. 978-1-4067-9706-0

British Library Cataloguing-in-publication Data
A catalogue record for this book is available
from the British Library.

Read Country Books
Home Farm
44 Evesham Road
Cookhill, Alcester
Warwickshire
B49 5lJ

www.readcountrybooks.com

CHAMPION LORD TOM NODDY OF BROADWAY

Owned by Mrs. EVELYN M. POWER

Winner of Nine Challenge Certificates

THE PUG-DOG

ITS HISTORY AND ORIGIN

BY

WILHELMINA SWAINSTON-GOODGER

WATMOUGHS LIMITED

IDLE AND LONDON

First Published 1930

PRINTED IN GREAT BRITAIN BY
MORRISON AND GIBB LTD., LONDON AND EDINBURGH

DEDICATED

TO

THE MEMORY OF

SWAINSTON GABRIELLE

A WORTHY MEMBER OF THE
"GRAND LITTLE BREED"

PREFACE

" At morning's call,
The small-voiced Pug-dog welcomes in the sun,
And flea-bit mongrels, wakening one by one,
Give answer all."

O. W. HOLMES.

THE pug-dog is one of the earliest breeds of dog—in
fact, so far as I can trace, it carries its history back
for a longer period than any other breed except the
greyhound. The greyhound is generally admitted,
without question, to be the earliest extant type of dog,
and J. Maxtee, in his *Popular Toy-Dogs : Their Breeding,
Exhibition and Management*, published in 1922, upholds
this theory when writing of pug-dogs :

" Pugs are of far more ancient date than is popularly
supposed. . . . There is ample existing evidence of this
in the museums and elsewhere, on the sculptures, etc. ;
and although I am not inclined to say that they are as
old as the Greyhound, I nevertheless favour the idea
that for antiquity such dogs run the latter very close—
so close, in fact, that it is difficult to separate the one from
the other in point of age."

So far as England is concerned there are few breeds
having so long an historical connection with this country,
being almost continually under Royal patronage ; and
they certainly appear to be the second oldest breed of
toy-dog, lap-spaniels of various denominations preceding
them.

With all breeds of dog the question of intelligence is
an important feature. Toy-dogs, having more of human

association, are in general more humanly intelligent than their outdoor brothers, which makes it difficult to draw a comparison between them. It would certainly be easier to train a young retriever to retrieve game than it would be to train a pug-dog to do so, whereat a sportsman might regard the retriever as being a more intelligent breed than the pug-dog ; but, in the house, as a house dog, the pug-dog admits no superiors. He is not only exceptionally quick of hearing but his bark, unlike many other toy-dogs, is a pleasing tone to the ear, being deep and full, which convinces a stranger that there is a big dog in the house ; and, he does not bark unless he means it. There is no continuous and useless yapping at the gate, for instance.

On the stage he has come into competition with the poodle, by many people given the name of being the most intelligent dog, because of his almost uncanny knack of learning tricks ; but the pug-dog has in many cases met and defeated the poodle on his own ground.

I certainly claim that there is no breed that can compete with the pug-dog in a question of general intelligence, especially in understanding the moods of his owner and accommodating himself to them—for either a tramp in the country or a *siesta* in front of the fire. He is ever ready when you are.

So far as popularity goes, he has twice been the most popular dog in England : once during the mid-eighteenth century, and once during the mid-Victorian era. The third time is approaching. He is, at present, the third most popular toy, so far as registrations [1] go, both in this country and in the U.S.A.

Until the coming of black pug-dogs in the late

[1] This book was chiefly written in 1928, and the registration figures, except when otherwise stated, are based upon the Kennel Club returns for 1927, and the American Kennel Club returns for 1926.

nineteenth century he was always a fawn-coloured dog with a black mask on his face, a black line, or trace, down his back, and a similar marking spreading across it at the shoulders known as a " saddle-mark." His fawn varied in shades, but the early specimens were golden or apricot fawns. Later the pepper-and-salts, or smutty fawns, were introduced. Tastes in a fancy change just as fashions do. At the present day the trace and saddle-mark are not so much insisted upon. These points were always more marked in the pepper-and-salts, or Willoughbys, as they used to be called. As far as fawns are concerned, the clear fawns, or Morrisons of the old day, seem to be the most favoured at the present time. We may have lost some of the trace and saddle-mark, but modern breeders have certainly succeeded in producing shorter faces without altering the noble character of the head.

It is very remarkable that the pug-dog should have kept up its distinctive form for so long. There is no difference between the earliest specimens and those of the present day, apart from improvements brought about by better conditions and selective breeding. There is not, I believe, one other breed of dog of which the same thing can be said. Many breeds have kept to distinctive types but few, if any, to distinctive details. It is really remarkable that in any breed any distinction at all should have been kept up, as no real interest in the points of dogs or in their pedigrees was taken till the nineteenth century, when dog-shows first made their appearance. From after that date people were compelled to breed up to a definite type, and in many cases (alas, how many?) inbreeding was the only result.

The pug-dog may claim his distinctive type in that he always keeps aloof from other breeds. He is not courageous with other dogs, which is, in my opinion, a distinct advantage, and it is probably through this that he is so seldom inflicted with that canine scourge, distemper. For many years I have enjoyed the society of pug-dogs, and for some eight years I have been breeding them ; yet, I have never had a pug-dog with distemper, and, so far as I have heard, none of the puppies I have sold have suffered from that disease. A case in point is that of a four-months-old puppy of mine who went to some people in the south. They had an Airedale terrier which was suffering from distemper, though the fact was not discovered until the day before the arrival of the puppy. The Airedale was sent to the veterinary surgeon, but, apart from this, no process of disinfection or other precautions were taken. Yet, the puppy marched, as it were, straight into the Airedale's distemper-infected shoes and remained absolutely unscathed. I may add that the Airedale had been allowed the run of the house during the day, and that the pug-dog therefore lived and lay in exactly the same spots as had been lived and lain in by the sick dog. I do not, of course, claim that pug-dogs are immune from distemper ; they certainly are not, but it is rare amongst them.

As house dogs they are admirable. They are naturally clean and almost wholly free from " doggy " smell. There can be no question about them being excellent watch-dogs. One thing that is not generally known is that they are exceptionally hardy, and the way the breed has thrived in Russia proves that the cold does not daunt them. This does not mean that they can be treated without any consideration at all and be expected to survive. Pug-dogs, like other breeds, must be treated with discernment in accordance with their physical and mental individualities. It is a fact that outdoor kennelling has proved successful in the South of England, but, the happiness of the dog being considered, I would not personally advise this method with pug-dogs, for the best results. Another important point of advantage that the pug-dog possesses over all long-coated breeds is emphasised by our uncertain English climate ; his short coat can be dried in a minute, and his *toilette* is a matter which would never cause pricks of conscience to those busy people who, fond as they are of their pets, often have a hundred and one other things to do besides the grooming of their dogs. The pug-dog is always smart and trim, and he keeps sweet and clean without the number of baths required by some of the other breeds. Many pug-dog lovers prefer the weekly grooming (all that is necessary) and seldom, if ever, bath their pug-dogs at all.

The pug-dog, if I may say so, is almost too perfect in associationship with children. This, of course, is perhaps to the dog's disadvantage, but certainly to the child's advantage. The breed is very popular, especially with young children, their velvety softness and their obviously comical appearance makes a direct appeal to the child heart, and careful grown-ups will not need to think twice of the advantage possessed by the pug-dog in his cleanliness and freedom from smell (for which he is deservedly famous). Everybody knows the fame of the canine races in general for their love and complete understanding of children. It is as if they knew that man's child was their worshipped master's most precious possession, but, apart from this, there is a camaraderie between the child and the dog from which the man, even if he be the master, often finds himself excluded. The pug-dog's unfailing good nature and absolute devotion to the object of his affection makes him an ideal companion for the child. There have been cases where the pug-dog has suffered martyrdoms at the hands of a child sooner than retaliate, which seems very sad to me, although I am just as much child-lover as I am canine enthusiast.

In extracts in this book taken from a letter of Mr. Mayhew and from the works of Mr. Lee you will see that each of these gentlemen knew of pug-dogs with distinctly sporting turns of mind. I have a little black bitch who also thoroughly enjoys rabbiting, and who goes out shooting with my husband without being in the least gun-shy. This little dog was once lost for a week in December on the moors near Newcastle, sleeping out in the very frosty air. Apart from slight skin trouble, picked up on this outing, she suffered no ill-effects. More recently, in late October, she was caught by the foot in a rabbit snare on the Cheviot Hills, and though search was made for her all night she was not discovered till eight o'clock the next morning, being in the snare for roughly fifteen hours. Beyond a few tears and a great show of gratitude to the person who unsnared her she showed no ill-effects whatsoever. There could hardly have been a better example of the hardiness of the breed or of its patience under adverse circumstances.

Some breeders claim that the black pug-dog is hardier than the fawn. I think this is questionable, but I have given a rather amusing extract with regard to this, written under the pseudonym, " La Vedette," in the chapter on blacks. " La Vedette " is perfectly right in substance, regarding the fawn pug-dog's aversion to wet weather, though, I think, he rather exaggerates it. The fawn dog is much like the average human being in this respect. He likes his comfort. It is more the thought of the chilly outing that rankles. Once the walk has started he enjoys himself as much as any other dog. Like everything else, it is all a matter of habit. Fawn pug-dogs who are taken for a regular walk every day show little reluctance at leaving the room and fireplace, whereas those who are taken out at irregular intervals might well be sympathised with should they infer that a fine day would have been more suitable for the abandonment of their cosy corner ! However, this aspersion, if it is an aspersion, could never under any circumstances be cast on the blacks. Let it rain or snow, Mr. Black Pug-Dog is just as happy, and would not miss his walk for any storm. He has all the small child's passion for paddling in muddy puddles, but he comes back after his walk in the rain, glowing and full of vigour, his lovely jetty satin coat looking more beautiful than ever, after a brisk rub-down.

Considering the historical association of the pug-dog with this country it is really rather remarkable that no book has been published on the breed in England. The Americans have their book by Dr. Cryer, but, apart from references to the pug-dog in canine text-books, no book has been written on the breed, either descriptive or historical. This present little book is a very cursory history of the breed, but it is hoped that if it proves acceptable, a larger work might be undertaken, in which case, I would indeed be very grateful to readers who could send me any points of interest or anecdotes about the breed, to Swainston Kennels, Startforth, Barnard Castle, Co. Durham.

As will be seen, I have given, where possible, various opinions of people on the breed at various dates, and I have taken a great many extracts from their works, which will be acknowledged when they are quoted ; but, apart from this, I wish to express my particular thanks to the British Museum (Natural History Section) for the extreme courtesy and kindness they have always shown me, and the great trouble its members have put themselves to in supplying information. I also gratefully acknowledge help received from the Victoria and Albert Museum, the British Museum (the Department of British and Mediæval Antiquities Section), H.M. Office of Works, the Royal College of Surgeons, the Zoological Society of London, and from the many correspondents who have been so kind as to reply to questions I have written to various papers.

W. SWAINSTON-GOODGER.

CONTENTS

"Alsatians, indeed!" snorted a fat pug-dog through his ridiculously inadequate nose. "We'll show 'em!" And he threw off the woollen shawl in which he had reclined like some one simply thirsting for a fight.

"Perhaps I may not see the day when our respectable old English race will hunt Alsatians out of the country, but *you* will," and he turned round to a litter of corkscrew-tailed pups in the next cage.

"Wather, wather," yapped the youngsters, treading on each other's backs in their excitement.

"That's the spirit," approved the veteran.

The Daily Mirror, 1927.

His face is distinctly his fortune with other dogs. There is something about the pug complexion which depresses quite big dogs, and a favourite jest among pug pups is to look steadily at an Alsatian and watch him run for miles.—*Northern Dispatch*, 1930.

THE PUG-DOG:
ITS HISTORY AND ORIGIN

CHAPTER I

THEORIES AS TO THE ORIGIN OF THE BREED

> " My lady, in her parlour snug,
> Is still delighted with her pug."
>
> *Joseph the Book Man,* 1821.

THE pug-dog has for many years been regarded as having sprung in some way or other from the bulldog, and many of the older books on natural history dismiss him summarily with being " a bull-dog in miniature." The Lexiconists have mostly followed this example.

It is difficult to trace how and when this theory started, though it is probable that the similarity in appearance between the two breeds gave rise to it in the first place, despite the fact that when the pug-dog was first introduced in large numbers into England during the late seventeenth century, it was styled the Dutch Mastiff and not the Dutch Bull-Dog.

An examination of the skulls of a bull-dog and a pug-dog shows clearly that, so far as anatomy goes, there is no relationship whatever between them.

The pug-dog appears undoubtedly to be a relation of the mastiff. Both mastiffs and pug-dogs were known at an early date in China, and the pug-dog, certainly, and possibly the mastiff, owe their origin to that country, though the latter was known very early in Europe.

Even to-day the standard British Museum catalogue [1] describes the pug-dog as having a possible relationship to the bull-dog.

" The Pug, which is believed to take its name from the Latin *pugnus*, a fist (in allusion to its short and square face), is evidently related to the Mastiff and the Bull-dog, although this history of its descent is lost. It is believed, however, to have been originally produced in Holland, at a comparatively recent date. At any rate it was fashionable in that country in the time of King William III., by whom numerous specimens were brought to England, where the breed has ever since been popular. The Pug appears to have been always a fawn-coloured dog with a black face and curly tail ; but about the middle of the nineteenth century two distinct strains—the Willoughby and the Morrison—were established. The former was characterised by the cold stone-fawn colour, and the excess of black, which showed itself in the completely or nearly black head and in the presence of a large ' saddle-mark ' or wide ' traces.' The Morrison strain, on the other hand, had a richer and yellower fawn, with no extra blackness. The two strains are, however, now more or less completely blended. There is also a black breed, of very modern origin. Owing to the shortness of the jaws, the teeth of the Pug are crowded together, so much so that the premolar teeth frequently have their long diameter placed transversely instead of longitudinally. A similar feature often occurs in the skulls of Pekinese and Japanese Spaniels and other lap-dogs. The breed is represented by a specimen purchased in 1908." [2]

[1] *A Guide to the Domesticated Animals exhibited in the Central and North Walls of the British Museum (Natural History)*, 1908.

[2] In spite of the short face produced by modern breeders, which is the first point generally looked for and admired in a good pug-dog, it is interesting to note that present-day judges usually insist on

G. L. le Clerc Buffon, in his *Historie Naturelle*, published in 1750, who Rawdon B. Lee [1] describes as the most unreliable of naturalists and "whose word" according to "Stonehenge," "no man relies on," carries the bull-dog in miniature theory to even greater lengths when he describes how the bull-dog was imported into South Africa by the Hollanders, when the Cape was a Dutch settlement, where it became modified into the form of a pug-dog, and was reimported into Holland as a lady's pet !

The pug-dog and the bull-dog are, of course, entirely different in character, but the most decisive argument that can be brought against the theory of the pug-dog being a bull-dog in miniature is that the pug-dog is a very considerably older breed than the bull-dog, so far as historical traces go. " It has been suggested," writes Frederick Gresham,[2]

" that the Pug is of the same family as the Bull-dog, and that it was produced by a cross with this and some

even sets of teeth. A crowded mouth of teeth, or such teeth as are described above, should handicap any pug-dog in the show-ring. There is no reason why a pug-dog's teeth should not be as even as the best terrier's mouthful. Pug-dogs' teeth are usually stronger and bigger than those of other toy breeds, such as the pekinese and the pomeranian. Presumably animal dentistry was not so advanced in those days. It is usual, nowadays, to remove any milk teeth from a pup's mouth, should it have too many, which can easily be done by a qualified veterinary surgeon. However, I have seen modern pug-dogs with the shortest possible faces and perfectly even sets of teeth. These particular dogs' teeth had grown quite naturally and they had had none removed. Of course, it must be taken into consideration that we know more about feeding all dogs, and have better foods for them, than did our ancestors. All this plays a great part in the health of a dog's teeth. Even twenty years ago, when the above extract was written, doubtless the erroneous method of feeding pet-dogs on slops was still prevalent.

[1] *A History and Description of Modern Dogs*, 1894.
[2] *Cassell's New Book of the Dog*, edited by Robert Leighton.

other smaller breed. But this is improbable, as there is
reason to believe that the Pug is the older breed, and it
is known that it has been bred with the Bull-dog for the
anticipated benefit of the latter."

And the author of *The Sportsmans' Repository*, published
in the early part of the nineteenth century, treats the
matter in a lighter vein when he states :

"Another, and which we deem an inconsequent
conjecture on this most important affair of origination,
is the Pug being, according to certain sage conjecturists,
a sample or first-class mongrel, the production of a
commixture between the English Bull-dog and the
little Dane, a conjecture we feel inclined to define by
the figure *hysteron-proteron*, or setting the cart before the
horse. We hold the Pug to be of the elder house ; and
if at this perilous anti-parodial crisis we may venture at
a secular parody, the motto of the illustrious race of
Pugs ought to be, not we from Bulls, but Bulls from us."

The pug-dog has been known by various classifications, but none of them seem to throw any light on its
origin. It has generally been known as the *Canis fricator*,
and some naturalists have classified it as being one of
the four British dogs under the heading *Canis Anglicus*,[1]
though it is more correctly classified under the *Pugnaces*
group.

Edward C. Ashe, in his *Dogs : Their History and Development*, published in 1927, states :

"Dogs are members of that order of 'animals of
prey' known as Carnivora, which, with fifteen other
orders, belong to a class of animals feeding their young
by mammary glands, the Mammalia. The dogs . . .
are, however, members of that easily distinguished family,
the Canidæ.

[1] *E.g.* "The Naturalist's Library," *Mammalia*, Lieut.-Col. Chas.
Hamilton Smith, 1840.

"We find that the dog family . . . characterised on the whole by long and pointed muzzles except in some Eastern breeds such as the Japanese Spaniel, the Pug, and Pekinese. . . .
"If on the other hand domestic varieties have been bred from existing types of wolves, foxes and jackals, and have gradually . . . changed to what they are to-day, then we should get two or three marked races, the wolf-like, fox-like and jackal-like ; but this would not explain the Thibet Mastiff or Bloodhound type or the short-faced Pugs, Japanese Spaniels, unless their ancestral form of wild animal existed once and has died out."

This statement is extremely interesting, as it excludes the pug-dog from all other breeds except the Japanese spaniel, the pekinese (or Pekin spaniel), the bloodhound and the mastiff.

One cannot help agreeing that the pug-dog and the mastiff are similar in every material respect except in that of size, and there seems no doubt that they are members of a similar group, or family, though it is difficult to say with any authority whether the mastiff [1] was bred from the pug-dog or the pug-dog from the mastiff. From the slight evidence there is before us it would appear that the pug-dog is the older breed. It must be remembered that all wild animals have a tendency to decrease in size and all domesticated animals to increase.

On the question of the bloodhound I would not like to express an opinion, but I cannot help feeling that the Pekin and Japanese spaniel are wrongly classified with the pug-dog and mastiff, because it would appear from their apple-shaped skulls that neither of them are naturally short-faced dogs. Both appear in the past to have had their faces considerably shortened by selective breeding, or inbreeding, resulting in the curious forma-tion of their heads ; and I suggest that both these species

[1] I am referring, of course, to the Chinese mastiff.

started out on life's journey with faces as long and pointed as the small old English spaniels exhibited at the present day, whereas an examination of the skulls will irrefutably show that those of pug-dog and mastiff are both of the same square character, totally in contradiction to the contracted appearance of the bull-dog's skull. It has been stated that the present-day pug-dog's face has been shortened by improved breeding. It must be clearly understood, however, that in-breeding was never necessary for this purpose. The pug-dog's muzzle, though longer in the past, has always been naturally square and inclined to shortness.

There can be no question that the muzzle of a dog can be shortened by selective breeding. The pug-dog is itself an example of this, though it has always been a naturally short-faced dog. In comparison with the skull of a short-faced spaniel the skull of a pug-dog or a mastiff is comparatively square and flat.

It seems quite clear, therefore, that our search for the origin of the pug-dog must commence where we find pug-dogs and mastiffs in conjunction. This was in China, from whence nearly all the short-faced breeds of dog sprang.

But before going so far as China there is one theory about the origin of the pug-dog which must be noted, because, though it has never, so far as I am aware, been stated in print, it is a theory often discussed and taken as correct. It is important in that it deals definitely with the first introduction of the breed into England.

Since the war—the exact date I have been unable to ascertain—a certain sale of china was held in London of various specimens, amongst which was a very old mother-of-pearl model of a short-faced, curly-tailed dog said to have been taken from an early Egyptian tomb.

In about 1888 certain alterations were made in the old Post Office in London, and during the excavation for a new site the foundations were sunk twenty-seven feet deeper, and an old Roman wall was discovered, together with the remains of a Roman villa, amongst which were found some animal remains, including the skull of a small, short-faced dog.

Upon these two statements is based a theory that the pug-dog was known to the ancient Egyptians, and during the period of Roman invasion of Egypt, specimens were imported into Rome as pets and from thence were imported into Britain—the first pug-dog, therefore, being introduced into this country some time during the period of Roman occupation. One might even carry this argument farther and suggest that the first pug-dogs were imported direct from Egypt by the Carthaginian traders, who are said to have brought across the mastiff.

I have been unable to trace anything with respect to the Egyptian dog, though it could not have been of such ancient lineage as some of the holders of this theory are inclined to believe, as mother-of pearl was not used by the ancient Egyptians in their modelling; and even during the Roman occupation of Egypt, when certain mosaic models were made, mother-of-pearl was rarely, if ever, used. I do not wish to deny the possibility of such a model having been discovered, possibly made of mother-of-pearl-like material, because where there is smoke there is usually fire, and the fact of the discovery being so often mentioned makes me think that there may be "something in it"; but without sufficient details being supplied to trace the actual specimen I would not like to express an opinion, except that this single model cannot be taken to be conclusive evidence that the pug-dog was known to the ancient Egyptians.

The Roman skull is certainly of greater interest, but again does not prove conclusive without further evidence to support it. I cannot trace this skull or I would supply a photograph in conjunction with the skulls of pug-dogs and other short-faced animals of the present day.

There seems little doubt, however, that such a skull was discovered,[1] and if the description given is accurate it would appear to have been that of a pug-dog as that was the only short-faced dog of the period.   In a letter on the subject to the Zoological Society of London they informed me that :

" There is no doubt, however, that it " (the pug-dog) " existed many years before the Romans invaded Britain, and there seems to be no reason why they should not have been responsible for introducing it into this country."

Roman ladies were known to cherish lap-dogs as pets, and pomeranians and dogs from the islands of Melita in the Ægean, now known as Maltese, were particularly favoured.   General A. H. L. Fox Pitt-Rivers has also traced relics of turnspits, or dachshunds, as well as small retrievers.   But apart from this single skull, no pug-dogs.

Again, I would like to say that the evidence is not strong enough to accept the theory of this skull being definitely established as that of a pug-dog, or that the breed was introduced into this country by way of Rome.

So far as England is concerned the pug-dog was unknown until the end of the seventeenth century, though James Watson in *The Dog Book*, published in 1906, is bold enough to state, without advancing any proof for his contention :

" While we have credited Holland with the original possession of the pug, we are not prepared to advance

[1] " The dog was certainly found on the General Post Office site. . . ."—From *A letter from the British Museum.*

any proof of the statement. Indeed, there is more reason, so far as the proofs we have seen, to suppose that it is every bit as much English as Dutch, but we need further information on the subject."

Apart from the Roman skull there seems to be only one other trace of the pug-dog in England prior to the Dutch invasion. Of this W. D. Drury, in his *British Dogs*, published in 1903, writes : .

" Coming to more recent times, we find the dearth of specific information with regard to dogs quite as great as that which characterised pre-mediæval days ; while the representations of dogs upon monumental tombs are often so rude as to give but the slightest clue to the identity of the animals thereon depicted. Sometimes it is the Greyhound that is thus selected as an emblem of fidelity ; at others a spotted dog, it may be a Dalmatian of the period, and at yet others a lap-dog, by some considered to represent a Pug of the period— namely, the latter part of the fourteenth century."

There seems to be only one other source from whence the pug-dog is claimed to have been imported— Muscovy, or Russia.

For many years the pug-dog has been a favourite in Russia. " There is yet," states *The Sportsman's Repository*,

" an obscure but confident tradition, that Pugism had its origin in Muscovy ; which, being granted, we may not have been wide of the mark in tracing in it the form of the Arctic dog."

And E. C. Ash, in his *Dogs and How to Know Them*, published in 1925, says that :

" Hundreds of years ago Pug-dogs were a feature of the Moscow market ; fine specimens sold at one shilling each. Varieties are fawns, also blacks and light creams. A black mask in fawns is an advantage.

"Originating in China, this handsome toy-dog became very popular in England, and was kept by people of taste and refinement. A very old breed, likely to come popular again."

The theory that pug-dogs were imported from Russia is unquestionably correct. They were imported in large quantities from that country during the eighteenth and nineteenth centuries, but there is no trace of pug-dogs ever having been imported from Russia prior to the importation of pug-dogs from Holland.

Without further proof it is impossible to say that pug-dogs were known in this country before the seventeenth century, and we can therefore set out in our search for their origin, not as a bastard or in-bred bull-dog, but as an original species, in the country where there are the first traces of them—China.

CHAPTER II

CHINA

" A veritable pug of pugs, with large, soft, loving eyes."
The World, 1876.

THE pug-dog was a well-known and well-authenticated Chinese breed of dog. It is said to have had its origin in a place in China called Lo-Chiang in the district of Ssuchuan, and the name given to it by the Chinese was *Lo-chiang-sze*, or, more simply, *Lo-sze*.[1]

It is difficult to state with any accuracy when the breed first came into prominence in China, but it was probably during the Chou dynasty, and, possibly, during the reign of the lascivious Yu-wang, who succeeded the warlike Suan-wang (827–782 B.C.).

According to the Zoological Society of London

" the Pug-dog is known to be one of the oldest of breeds and originated in China some 700 years B.C."

whilst Edward C. Ash [2] states that

" the breed probably originated in China, and spread from there to Japan, and thence to Europe. In China short-mouthed dogs known as ' Lo-sze ' are mentioned in early native literature as far back as 700 B.C."

It is excessively difficult to say when the introduction of Chinese dogs into Japan commenced, but about

---

[1] This word used to be the name for " Russia " in Chinese.
[2] *Dogs : Their History and Development.*

A.D. 670 the Chinese and Japanese became interested in one another, and the Chinese presented the Japanese with small dogs which were regarded by the Japanese as being extremely valuable—so much so that when the Japanese Emperor demanded a tribute from China in A.D. 824, he included in his terms two Chinese *pai* [1] dogs as well as two of some other breed.

Again referring to Edward C. Ash, quoting from H. Ramsay's *Western Thibet*, published in 1890 :

" Chinese pug-dogs were also introduced as far as Lhasa.   In Thibetan they were called *lags k'yi* (*i.e.* hand dogs), because it was believed that if a human being lays his hand upon a young eagle when freshly hatched, the bird is transformed into a dog of the Chinese pug breed."

It was not until about A.D. 100 that dogs in China were given individual names.

Another rather amusing anecdote is given by Edward C. Ash, but he does not state as to what breed of dog he refers :

" From the official history of the Han dynasty (of A.D. 168–90) we learn that the Emperor Ling Ti was exceedingly interested in breeding dogs.   To one kept in his western garden at Lo Yang (Honan-fu), he gave the official hat of the Chin Hsien grade, which, we read, was one of the most important literary ranks of the period.   The hat was 8¾ inches high in front, 3¾ inches high behind, and 10 inches broad.   Other dogs held other ranks, whilst females had the ranks to which wives of officials were entitled."

The Pekin spaniel probably sprang from the pug-dog by way of the short-coated Chinese Happa-dog.   The Happa-dog is not well known in England, but there is an excellent stuffed specimen in the British Museum

[1] Any type of small, short-legged and small-headed dog.

(Natural History Section), and it is not uncommon in the United States. Under the heading "Happa" in W. E. Mason's *Dogs of All Nations*, published in 1915, it is described as follows :

"The Happa is identical in every respect with the Pekinese Spaniel, except that his coat is short and smooth."

One must be very careful not to confuse the Chinese Happa-dog with the Dutch *Happa-hond*, which is the term used in that country to describe a pug-dog.

Another confusion which arises over this Happa-dog is that, according to B. Lanfer, there was in Turkey

"a small and alert class" (of dog) "called *ha-pa* dogs."

It is difficult to say whether these Turkish *ha-pa* dogs were the same as Chinese Happa-dogs or a distinct breed altogether, or whether it was from Turkey, and not from China, that the pug-dog was imported, and the Dutch term of *Happa-hond* applied to the breed was merely another form of the Turkish *ha-pa*.

Toy-dogs appear to have become prominent in court circles during the Tang dynasty, according to the late Chinese minister, Lord Li Ching-fong, who wrote in *The Pekingese*, edited by Lillian C. Smythe :

"Toy dogs first became popular in the Tang Dynasty, that is, about the eighth century (Christian era), and again in the Sung Dynasty (eleventh century)."

Chinese legend tells us that the pekinese sprang from a mating between a marmoset and a lion, and though the dog, the Pekin spaniel, was common enough in China, certain specimens were kept in the royal palace and were regarded as sacred.

The Pekin spaniel was imported into Europe at an

early date, and Mrs. Lilburn MacEwen in 1904 stated that they were known to the Court of Henri III., and came to the Court of our Charles II. Apparently they did not reach the United States until Mrs. Eva B. Guyer obtained a specimen from Europe in 1898.

The importation of the sacred Palace[1] dog did not take place till late in the nineteenth century. Lady Algernon Gordon-Lennox, writing in *Cassell's New Book of the Dog*, states that :

" The history of the breed in England dates from the importation in 1860 of five dogs taken from the Summer Palace, where they had, no doubt, been forgotten on the flight of the Court to the interior. Admiral Lord John Hay, who was present on active service, gives a graphic account of the finding of these little dogs in a part of the garden frequented by an aunt of the Emperor, who had committed suicide on the approach of the Allied Forces. Lord John and another naval officer, a cousin of the late Duchess of Richmond's, each secured two dogs ; the fifth was taken by General Dunne, who presented it to Queen Victoria. Lord John took pains to ascertain that none had found their way into the French camp, and he heard then that the others had all been removed to Jehal with the Court. It is therefore reasonable to suppose that these five were the only Palace dogs, or Sacred Temple dogs of Pekin, which reached England, and it is from the pair which lived to a respectable old age at Goodwood that so many of the breed now in England trace their descent.

" Many years ago Mr. Alfred de Rothschild tried, through his agents in China, to secure a specimen of the Palace dog for the writer, in order to carry on the Goodwood strain, but without success, even after a correspondence with Pekin which lasted more than two years ; but we succeeded in obtaining confirmation of what we had always understood : namely, that the

---

[1] The Palace dog was rigorously conserved to one uniform uni-coloured type of sleeve dog, always having a dark red coat and black mask.

Palace dogs are rigidly guarded, and that their theft is punishable by death. At the time of the Boxer Rebellion, only Spaniels, Pugs, and Poodles were found in the Imperial Palace when it was occupied by the Allied Forces, the little dogs having once more preceded the Court in the flight to Signanfu."

It will be seen from this account that pug-dogs were still kept as pets in the royal palace at Pekin as late as the end of last century.

No paintings or models of the pekinese type of dog, dating from earlier than the nineteenth[1] century, are known to exist.

Again referring to Edward C. Ash, I find that :

" There are considerable numbers of references to dogs in early chronicles. The Emperor Ren Tsung, about A.D. 1041, was faced by a mutiny of his palace troops. One of the officials (a censor) advised him that he ought to keep a dog. ' In Ssuchuan there is a place named Lo-chiang famous for its dogs. Search should be made for one of these having a red coat and a short tail. Such as these are very quick of ear and should be bred in the palace so as to give early warning of trouble outside.' The enemies of this censor, whose name was Sung, nicknamed him ' Sung Lo-chiang,'[2] for giving the Emperor this advice."

It is interesting to note that the pug-dog was even recognised in those days as being the best watch-dog— a title which he proved to be his with William of Orange, and one which every person knowing the breed will admit at the present day. With regard to the colour I can only suggest that there has been a mistake in the translation, or that the pug-dogs of that day were of a ruddier shade of fawn.

Dogs, both in China and Japan, were treated with

[1] V. W. F. Collier, *Dogs of China and Japan.*
[2] The nickname approximately means " Pug-dog Sung."

an almost exaggerated consideration, and the smaller the breed the more highly it was prized. Kaempfer refers to dogs in Japan about 1727, when he tells how they

"went by the place where publick orders and proclamations were put up, not far from the ditch of the castle, where we saw a new proclamation put up lately and twenty shuits of silver nail'd to the post to be given as a reward to any body that would discover the accomplice of a murder lately committed upon a dog."

In *A Journey to the Tea Countries of China*, by R. Fortune, published in 1852, a description is given of the toy-dogs of Japan :

" The lap-dogs of the country are highly prized both by natives and by foreigners. They are small—some of them not more than 9 or 10 inches in length. They are remarkable for sunk-noses and sunken eyes, and are certainly more curious than beautiful. They are carefully bred ; they command high prices even amongst the Japanese ; and are dwarfed, it is said, by the use of saki—a spirit to which their owners are particularly partial. Like those of the larger breed already noticed, they are remarkable for the intense hatred they bear to foreigners."

G. R. Jesse, in his *Researches into the History of the British Dog*, published in 1866, refers to the above extract, and writes :

" The author expresses some surprise that the dogs share the antipathies of their masters. Does he not know that the animal is not only the most sincere, but the staunchest of friends ? None can say of him : ' Out on this half-faced fellowship ! ' for our friends, are his friends ; our enemies, his enemies."

The date of the first importation of pug-dogs from China or Japan direct to this country is lost, but certainly there was a good trade from China in pug-dogs during the early part of the nineteenth century, as the first Kennel Club Stud Book shows by entry : " Click, by Lamb (from Pekin) out of Moss."

The exaggerated pampering applied to toy-dogs in Japan resulted in the degeneration of the species. In China the dogs were treated with much more common sense. Edward Richard Lydekker, in his *Royal Natural History*, published in 1893, gives a description of a pug-dog imported from Japan :

" The Chinese, or, as it is often incorrectly called from being imported into Japan and thence brought to Europe, the Japanese pug, is a still more extraordinary animal, exhibiting a kind of degradation from over breeding. One of these brought to England about 1867 was a slender-legged animal with very long hair, and the bushy tail closely curled over its back. The face was extremely short, and the jaws very feeble, with only a single pair of incisor teeth in the lower one. This pug lived chiefly on vegetables and exhibited a special partiality for cucumber."

CHAPTER III

HOLLAND

" Then half arose
His little pug-dog with his little pug-nose."
R. H. BARHAM, *Ingoldsby Legends,* 1840.

THE following query was inserted in *Notes and Queries,*
second series, vol. v., on p. 131, for the year 1858.
It received no replies :

" *The Prince of Orange's Dog.* Sir Roger Williams,
in his *Actions of the Lowe Countries* (printed by Humfrey
Lownes, for Mathew Lownes, 1618), 4to, p. 49, gives
an interesting account of a Camisado, or night attack,
by Julian Romero upon the camp of the Prince of Orange,
in which the Prince's life was saved by a dog :

" ' For I heard the Prince say often, that as hee
thought, but for a dog he had been taken. The Camisado
was given with such resolution, that the place of armes
tooke no alarme, untill their fellowes were running in
with the enemies in their tailes. Whereupon this
dogge, hearing a great noyse, fell to scratching and crying,
and withall leapt on the Prince's face, awaking him
being asleep, before any of his men. And albeit the
Prince lay in his armes, with a lackey alwaies holding
one of his horses ready bridled ; yet at the going out of
his tent, with much adoe hee recovered his horse before
the enemie arrived. Nevertheless one of his Quiries
was slaine taking horse presently after him ; and divers
of his servants were forced to escape amongst the guards
of foote, which could not recover their horses. For
truth, ever since, untill the Prince's dying day, he kept
one of that dog's race ; so did many of his friends and

followers. The most or all of these dogs were white little
hounds, with crooked noses, called Camuses.'

" The fashionable lap-dog of the days of the first
two Georges was the ugly little Dutch pug. It was
also customary to decorate them with *orange*-coloured
ribbons.

" *Query :* Is the origin of this fashion to be traced to
Sir Roger Williams' anecdote ?

" EDWARD F. RIMBAULT."

To this query I answer " Yes."

In giving this answer I am treading on rather
dangerous ground, for Captain A. H. Trapman has
recently thrown a bomb-shell into the world of pugdom
by describing the dog as a spaniel—a contention I have
never heard before from a writer on canine matters.

Two historians of modern days have certainly
described the dog to be a spaniel, but without giving
any authority, and their statements have always been
regarded, as far as I have heard, in the canine world
as incorrect as to the breed of the dog ; and every
leading writer on dogs who has mentioned the incident
has invariably given the palm for saving the Prince at
Hermigny to the pug-dog. The result seems also to
prove the contention, for the pug-dog was adopted as
the favourite breed of the house of Orange from ever
after the battle, and became widely popular throughout
the whole of the Netherlands.

To give a careful consideration of the question it
is necessary to set out several accounts of the battle.
The most important, because it is the earliest and is
written by a contemporary writer, is that of Sir Roger
Williams, Kt., part of which has been set out in Mr.
Rimbault's query :

" The Prince being retyred into his Campe, *Julian
Romero* with earnest perswasions procured licence of
Duke *d'Alva*, to hazard a Camisado that night upon

the Prince. At midnight *Julian* sallyed out of the trenches with a thousand musketiers, and two thousand armed men, most pikes ; all the rest stood in armes in the trenches, their horsemen ready without the trenches to second *Julian*, principally for his retreite if need were. *Julian* divided his forces into three troupes. The first two hundred olde shot, which could keepe their matches close, led by a desperate Captaine named *Muncheco*. The second one thousand armed men and shot, led by *Julian* himselfe. The third led by his Lieutenant Collonell and Sergeant Maior ; whom he commanded to stand fast in the midst of their way betwixt the two Campes for his retriete ; and not to stir unlesse some of credit came from him to Command the contrarie. Presently after his directions, he commanded *Muncheco* to charge ; who resolutely forced two guards, being at the least a regiment of *Almaines*. *Julian* seconded with all resolution, in such sort, that hee forced all the guards that he found in his way into the place of armes before the Prince's tent. Here he entered divers tents ; amongst the rest his men killed two of the Prince's secretaries hard by the Prince's tent, and the Prince himselfe escaped very narrowly."

Sir Roger's account continues in the words set out in Mr. Rimbault's query.

Ruth Putnam, the American historian, in his *William the Silent, Prince of Orange*, published in 1895, describes the action as follows :

" On the night of 11th September,[1] Julian Romero led a small force of six hundred men to Hermigny. The night was dark, and they had put their shirts outside of their armour to distinguish each other in the obscurity. Silently as snow they succeeded in surprising the sentinels, cutting them down like grass, and thus gained a way into the sleeping camp. Orange heard no noise, and slept quietly on until aroused by a little spaniel that was sleeping at his feet. Not content with

[1] 1572.

barking, the little creature licked his master's face. The Prince sprang out of bed, seized a horse that was ready saddled, and rode off in the darkness."

The third account contains extracts from Motley, and is taken from the valuable book of Miss Estelle Ross, published in 1924 under the title of *The Book of Noble Dogs.*"

" The Reformation, which the Earl of Wiltshire's dog hastened in England, was marked in Holland, then under Spanish yoke, by persecution. The Dutch patriots, of whom William, Prince of Orange, was leader, were reformers, and they headed a national rising against their oppressors.

" At one time the Spanish army was within half a league of Prince William's encampment at Hermigny, and the Spanish commander, Julian de Romero, determined on a surprise attack on the Dutch camp. Six hundred musketeers, their shirts over their armour to distinguish one another in the darkness, made a sortie and reached their objective without any alarm having been raised. ' The sentinels were cut down, the whole army surprised, while, for two hours long, from one o'clock in the morning till three, the Spaniards butchered their forces.'

" While this tumult was afoot, it is somewhat surprising that no sound roused the Prince of Orange and his attendants. One alone awoke to the danger—the little pug-dog Pompey, who slept on his bed. ' This creature,' Motley writes in *The Rise of the Dutch Republic,* ' sprang forward at the sound of hostile footsteps, and scratched his master's face with his paws. There was but just time for the Prince to mount a horse, which was ready saddled, and to effect his escape through the darkness before his enemies sprang into the tent. His servants were cut down, the master of his horse, and two of his secretaries, who gained their saddles a moment later, all lost their lives, and but for the little dog's watchfulness, William of Orange, upon whose shoulders the whole weight of his country's fortunes depended, would have been led within a week to an ignominious death.'

"The Prince himself frequently acknowledged his indebtedness : ' but for my little dog I should have been killed.'

"There is doubt whether Pompey perished that day, or whether, as Freville, with what authority we cannot trace, states, he lived and was a second time instrumental in saving his master's life, remaining with him till its close, when he defied the undertaker's men to lay the body in the coffin.

"One thing is certain : from that day forward the Prince was never without a pug sleeping on his bed ; and where he sleeps in effigy in Delft Cathedral one lies at his feet.

"When William III. came to the throne of England, Dutch pugs, decked with yellow ribbons, became fashionable pets in honour of the house of Orange."

Both Motley and Putnam describe the dog as a spaniel; but both are modern historians, not writers on canine matters, and breeds of dogs were very confused in the sixteenth century. I would prefer to rely on the description given by Sir Roger. The word *Camus* is French, and means "flat-nosed." Gilpin, R.A., as early as 1798, described them as "Dutch Pugs."

Spaniels were a well-known breed in England at that date, though there were certainly no short-faced varieties. The name, of course, comes from "Espaignol," meaning Spanish, and the breed was referred to in England as far back as Chaucer.[1] It is remarkable, therefore, that if Sir Roger meant a spaniel he should not have said a spaniel. He is apparently at a loss to describe this new specimen of the canine species, and he merely calls it the "white ' flat-nosed.' " The word " white " can be taken to mean light of colour.

[1] " For, as a spaynel, she wol on hym lepe" (Chaucer, 1386). "A goode spaynel shulde not be rough, but his taile shulde be rough" (*Master of Game*, 1410).

Idstone (the Rev. T. Pearce) bears out these theories in his book, *The Dog*, published in 1872 :

"The Pug was most fashionable about 1702, and especially from the time of William III. to George II. He was decorated with orange ribbons ; and the reasons for William's partiality to the breed are given in a scarce book called *Sir Roger Williams : His Actions of the Low Countries* (1618). This book states : ' The Prince of Orange being retired into camp, Julian Romero procured the licence of the Duke of D'Alva to hazard a camisado or night attack on the prince. Julian sallied out with a thousand pikemen, found their way to the prince's tent, and killed two of his secretaries. The prince's dog fell to scratching, and awakened him : and ever after the prince kept a dog of the breed. They are not remarkable for their beauty, being little white dogs, with crooked, flat noses, called " Camuses "—Camus meaning " flat-nosed." ' Gilpin, R.A., in 1798, called them ' Dutch Pugs.' I have no doubt that the ' white ' dogs mentioned above were drab or granite-coloured dogs of a light tint."

Rawdon B. Lee, too, gives the story, and states that :

"History tells us that the pug became first favourite at the Dutch Court,"

after the incident which he describes in terms very similar to those quoted above ; and, again, Edward C. Ash and V. W. F. Collier [1] follow his example.

I have myself heard the pug-dog referred to in Germany as " The Lutherean dog," because, by this incident, it was said to have been the cause of the continuance of the reformation in Europe ; and the Church of England certainly owes its existence to the pug-dog for, had the house of Orange failed, there would have been no Protestant champion to take

[1] *Dogs of China and Japan.*

over the throne after England had relapsed under James II.

The arms of our bishops should be supported by a pug-dog on one side and a spaniel on the other, for it was certainly a spaniel belonging to Lord Wiltshire which was, according to Foxe, one of the chief causes of the breach of this country with Rome.

There seems to me to be no possibility of doubt that it was a pug-dog which saved William of Orange.

But in the first place, how did the pug-dog get to Holland ?

The Portuguese and Spaniards were trading with the East during the early part of the sixteenth century, but the Dutch certainly were not.

The battle of Hermigny was fought in 1572, and pug-dogs must have been in Holland before that time. Now the *Oostindische Vereenigde Maatschappij*, which was afterwards known as the Dutch East India Company, was not formed until the 20th of March 1602, so all the statements that have so often been made to the effect that it was this company which imported the pug-dog are erroneous. In fact, no Dutch ship sailed to the East before the 2nd of April 1595, when an expedition set out under Cornelius Houtman. However, before the union between Spain and Portugal in 1580 the Dutch had been the chief carriers of Eastern produce from Lisbon to Northern Europe, and it is probable that the first pug-dogs were brought from China by the Spanish, or, more probably, Portuguese ships, about the beginning of the sixteenth century; and the dogs were then purchased by the Dutch sailors and reshipped to Holland, by whom they were, apparently, at first named *Camuses*, because of their peculiar appearance, and, later, *happa-honds*.

William of Orange was, no doubt, presented with one of these new arrivals by his sailors, which he called

Pompey; and after the battle of Hermigny they immediately became popular, not only with the Court, but with the whole people of Holland.

This is rather remarkable, as there seems to be no records of pug-dogs being known in Spain during the sixteenth century. There was certainly one theory I heard which connected the pug-dog with the Spanish Court. It has been said that the pug-dog was popular at the Court of Ferdinand and Isabella, and that because of this they were known as " Isabelleans," which explains the fact that many of the early female specimens of the breed were named Bella, just as many of the male specimens were called Pompey. I cannot trace any proof that the pug-dog was known to the Court of Ferdinand and Isabella, and I believe the name Isabelleans arose from a very different source.

In France fawn colour is known as Isabelle—the colour so called is the yellow of soiled calico.[1] The word arose from a vow made by Isabel of Austria (d. 1633), daughter of Philip II. of Spain, at the siege of Ostend, not to change her linen till the fort was captured. The siege lasted three years ! A similar story is told of Isabella of Castile at the siege of Granada. This may possibly explain the term " Isabellean " being applied to pug-dogs at a time when the black variety were unknown.

William III. of Nassau, Prince of Orange, posthumous son of William II., Prince of Orange, and of Mary, daughter of Charles I. of England, grandson of William I., Prince of Orange, who was saved by his pug-dog Pompey, was born in 1650. He married Mary, eldest daughter of James II. of England, and suc-

---

[1] " His colour was isabel, a name given in allusion to the whimsical vow of Isabella Clara Eugenia, Governess of the Netherlands, at the memorable siege of Ostend, which lasted from 1601 till 1604 " (Dillon : *Travels in Spain* (1781)).

ceeded to the stadtholdership of the Netherlands in 1672. He landed at Torbay in England on the 5th November 1688, and was crowned as William III. on the 11th of April 1689. And with him when he landed were his *happa-honds*, which came over from Holland in large numbers as part and parcel of his retinue.

Thus, late in the year 1688, the first known contingent of pug-dogs honoured this country with their arrival.

I cannot omit a reference to the somewhat vexed question of the pug-dog in Dutch art. There are a considerable number of Dutch pictures containing pug-dogs, and also Dutch ware, particularly mugs, was often decorated with a pug-dog's head.

" Many an old Dutch jug," writes E. C. Ash in his *Dogs and How to Know Them*,

" shows strange and often grotesque specimens of the Pug-dog, dancing on its hind legs to music."

James Watson, mentioning the subject, states that :

" In the Bloomfield Moore collection of pottery in Centennial Hall, Philadelphia, we saw a good many years ago a cropped pug with two puppies in Delft ware, which was dated as seventeenth-century production ; but on making inquiry regarding it, for the purpose of illustration, investigation was made, and it was found that the date given was wrong, and it is not believed to be over one hundred years old."

Mr. Watson, in his interesting article on pug-dogs in early Dutch art, failed to find in the New York collection any early picture or ware containing representation of pug-dogs. These early paintings and ware illustrated by Dutch pug-dogs are so often referred to, that when I noticed the following sentence :

" In many of the paintings of the old Dutch and Flemish masters, dogs of unmistakable Pug type may be seen as accessories in pictures of domestic life."

in an article by Mr. Robert Leighton in *The Dog World*, for the 8th of February 1929, I asked my husband to write to *The Dog World*, so that we might have the opinion of this established authority on the question, and Mr. Leighton very kindly replied in the same paper on the 22nd of February 1929, as follows :

" The Dog in Art

" Referring to my article on the origin of the Pug, which appeared in *The Dog World* of 8th February, Mr. C. J. S. Goodger asks me to state definitely the name of any Dutch paintings in which the Pug is represented. I am afraid I cannot supply him with precise information concerning individual pictures ; but it is a habit of mine, when visiting Continental art galleries, to make note of early paintings in which dogs of recognisable breed are introduced, and I have come upon several such paintings representing small dogs of Pug type in the galleries of Brussels, Amsterdam, The Hague, and Copenhagen.

" I especially remember one by Gabriel Metzu (1630–1667) in the Hermitage collection at Petrograd, in which an unmistakable Pug is very accurately treated by an artist, who evidently understood the characteristics of the breed. From this circumstance it is to be judged that the Pug was a familiar breed in Holland during the seventeenth century, and probably earlier.

" I regret that I cannot particularise, but I do not preserve my notes or keep the catalogues after they have served their purpose of helping me to trace the history of the different canine breeds. I can only assure Mr. Goodger that my statement was not made at random. The old Flemish and Dutch masters were very fond of introducing dogs as accessories in their pictures of domestic life, as any one may realise who visits the loan collection of Dutch art now being exhibited at Burlington House."

CHAPTER IV

ENGLAND

"A fine Lady . . . keeps a Pug-dog, and hates the Parsons."
D. Garrick : *Lethe*, 1749.

DURING the Tudor period in England pet dogs were not generally cultivated, people being more partial to the larger breeds of hunting dogs ; whilst, as ever in England, the oldest British breed of dog, the mastiff, was widely kept. In the reign of Henry VIII. strict laws were passed, forbidding dogs being brought to Court, so that his palaces might be

"swete, wholesome, cleane, and well furnished as to a prince's house and state doth apertyne."

Henry himself, however, was above his laws, and had great partiality for his two dogs, Cutte and Belle, and also, it is said, for the two turnspits of his palace, Hob and Nob. Spaniels, too, were popular during this reign, the most famous being that belonging to the Earl of Wiltshire, which was hacked to death by the Swiss Guard in the Vatican.[1]

[1] "Howbeit one thing is not here to be omitted, as a prognosticate of our separation from the See of Rome, which then chanced by a spaniel of the Earl of Wiltshire, which came out of England with him, and stood directly between the Earl and the Bishop of Rome, when the said Bishop had advanced forth his feet to be kissed. Now whether the spaniel perceived the Bishop's foot of another nature than it ought to be, and so taking it to be some kind of repast—or whether it was the will of God to show some token by a dog unto the bishop of his inordinate pride, that his feet were

James V. of Scotland, Henry's contemporary, showed great favour for his hunting dogs, Basche and Bawtie, and every one knows the story of the fidelity of the little spaniel[1] belonging to his ill-fated daughter, Mary, Queen of Scots.

Mary's son, who ascended the throne of England under the title of James I., inherited his mother's love for dogs—though, again, his affection was for dogs of a large breed, and particularly for his dog named Jewell, who was accidentally shot by his queen. His son, Charles I., divided his affection between his greyhound Gipsey and Prince Rupert's white poodle, Boye, who lost his life at Marston Moor. In this reign it was said that greyhounds were the kings of dogs, spaniels were gentlemen and hounds but yeomen. It was, of course, before the arrival in Britain of the pug-dog, because, if he had been there at this time, I am sure he would have been the emperor of dogs.

Charles II., as all the world knows, went in entirely —after the Restoration—for the toy spaniels which bear his name; whilst James II. is said not to have scrupled to sacrifice the lives of his sailors to save his favourite dog, Mumper.

In these reigns the fashions of the people chiefly followed those set by their sovereigns.

But from the time of the Stuart accession dogs were not the only animals kept as pets, and, particularly in the reign of the second Charles, monkeys, which were then called pugs, vied with the small dogs for the favour of the great ladies of the land. Notices frequently appeared

more meet to be bitten of dogs than kissed of Christian men—the spaniel . . . went directly to the Pope's feet, and not only kissed the same unmannerly, but, as some plainly reported and affirmed, took fast with his mouth the great toe of the Pope, so that in haste he pulled in his glorious feet from the spaniel : whereat our men, smiling in their sleeves, what they thought God knoweth" (Foxe).

[1] Some say, Skye terrier.

in the news-sheets of the time, such as : " Lady So-and-so was seen in the Mall followed by her page carrying her pug."

The word " pug " is of considerable antiquity in England, and is derived from the word " puck " meaning an " imp " or " fairy." In early days it was used purely as a term of endearment :

" If in a couche, a fyne fleesde lambe a kinge shoulde cause to ryde. And geve it rayments neate and gay and call it pugges and prety peate."

T. DRANT, 1566.

" My sweete pugge . . . thi absens will make the returne of thy swete cumpany the more welcum to me."

Sir G. CAREY, 1580.

" I have had foure husbands my selfe. The first, I called, sweet duck : the second, deare heart, the third, prettie pugge."

ANTONIO's *Revenge*, 1602.

" My prettie Pug (so fooles, hugging their bables, tearme them)."

RANDLE COTGRAVE, 1611.

About the time of the accession of the house of Stuart, the word " pug " used as a term of endearment seems to have gone out of fashion, and was applied as a name to the small monkeys that were then being imported. I have little doubt that the word was the same as that used as a term of endearment and was not, as has so often been stated, a new word coined from the Latin *pugnus* (meaning " a fist "), taken from the fact that the shadow of a pug's head on a wall resembled a clenched fist.

All the following quotations, which have over and over again been quoted in proof of the early arrival of pug-dogs in this country, do not refer to pug-dogs but to pugs :

" A little puppie, or pug to play with."
RANDLE COTGRAVE, 1611.

" Pugs and Baboons may claim a Traduction from Adam as well as these." H. POWER, 1664.

" As if he had sent his Lady Apess with a puglet or two to have squeal'd and scream'd at us."
T. FLATMAN, 1681.

" The monkey by chance came jumping out with them. . . . Poor Pug was had before his betters."
J. CRULL, 1698.

" Poor Pug was caught, to town conveyed. There sold. How envied was his doom. Made captive in a lady's room." J. GAY.

—whilst the word " pug," used by Ben Jonson in " The Devil is an Ass " in 1616, and the following quotation from Samuel Butler in 1664 refers to the word " pug " in its pure meaning of " puck," an imp or fairy :

"AGRIPPA'S PUG

" Quoth Hudibras—
Agrippa kept a Stygian pug
I' th' garb and habit of a dog,
That was his tutor, and the cur
Read to th' occult philosopher,
And taught him subtly to maintain
All other sciences are vain."

All these proofs that the pug-dog was known in England before the reign of William III. whittle away when the full texts are considered.

As a matter of fact, the earliest English reference to the pug-dog in print that I can trace does not appear to be before Bailey wrote, *Pug, a Nickname for a Monkey or Dog*, in 1731 ; and even as late as the time of Samuel

Johnson, the word " pug " is referred to as meaning a monkey, and the word " pug-dog " is not mentioned :

" *Pug.*—A kind name of a monkey, or any thing tenderly loved. (' Upon setting him down, and calling him *pug*, I found him to be her favourite monkey.'— ADDISON.) " [1]

Idstone furnishes a different theory altogether and takes the name from the Greek :

" I have stated, in an article written by me for the *Field Newspaper*," he writes, " that this dog derives its name from the Greek word πυξ whence comes the Latin *pugnus*, ' a fist,' because the shadow of a clenched fist was considered to resemble the dog's profile."

This theory of Idstone was attacked by Hugh Dalziel in his *British Dogs*, published in 1888, with, I think, some effect ; but I cannot accept his suggestion set out at the end of the quotation.

" As to the origin of the name, ' Idstone '—a writer always prone to travel miles out of the way to drag in a fanciful or obscure word or meaning, rather than use the commonplace one that stares everybody in the face— says " :

He gives the quotation set out above, and continues :

" I call that learned nonsense, because there is not a vestige of proof advanced, or to be advanced, in support of it. It would have been a more reasonable suggestion that the dog was named Pug because of being short and thick set."

Pug-dogs immediately came into popularity with the accession of William III., and, as they rose in favour, so did the pugs sink, and finally disappeared. The new

[1] *Johnson's Dictionary.*

breed on its introduction was called Dutch Mastiffs or, more commonly, Dutch Pugs, because their wrinkled masks were thought to resemble the faces of the pugs of the day. When the pugs ceased altogether to be fashionable, the prefix " Dutch " was dropped, and the breed began to be called simply " pugs," or, more correctly, " pug-dogs."

The dogs of this time were light fawns, rather larger in size than those bred at present, with dark masks, a more clearly defined trace, and certainly longer in the face than those which would be accepted nowadays. Their tails were tightly curled and their ears cropped close to the head. I have been unable to ascertain when cropping the ears commenced, but this disfigurement continued to be seen up to the present century, despite the protests of Idstone in 1872.

" In the old days it would have been impossible to have found a good specimen uncropped, but the remonstrances of judges and purchasers had their effect, and all the best dogs shown had their ears as nature made them, until the exhibition of 1871, at the Crystal Palace, where, I regret to say, several mutilated specimens were exhibited.

" The reason assigned for thus disfiguring them is an exceedingly weak one, that it, ' adds to the puckers or wrinkles in the forehead ' : but this is not true ; in fact, it has a tendency to draw the skin of the forehead tight. I would never myself give a prize to any Pug-dog thus tortured if there were one unmutilated in the class which could be called a fair example ; and I trust that all judges will discountenance the exercise of these barbarous customs."

Some extraordinary views were held as to the requisites of the pug-dog when it was first introduced into this country, amongst which was the belief that the tongue should protrude from the mouth—a blemish

3

which we now know to be caused through partial paralysis of that organ. Another was that the tails of female pug-dogs were not considered correct unless they were curled on the opposite side of the back to those of a male.[1]

"About the time Hogarth, the great painter, flourished," writes Rawdon B. Lee, "Dutch pugs were as fashionable as black pages, and no lady of title was considered to be fully equipped unless she had both in her following."

The sudden popularity of the new breed and its curious appearance immediately excited the caricaturists of the time, who were particularly prolific during the days of the Georges, and especially during the rebellions of 1715 and 1745; and the great people of the land, who nearly all kept pug-dogs, were continually finding themselves caricatured with pug-dog faces.

J. G. Wood, in his *Illustrated Natural History*, published in 1851, writes concerning him :

"The Pug-dog is an example of the fluctuating state of fashion and its votaries. Many years ago the Pug was in a very great request as a lap-dog or ' toy ' dog, as these little animals are more correctly termed. The satirical publications of the last century are full of sarcastic remarks upon Pug-dogs and their owners, and delighted in the easy task of drawing a parallel between the black-visaged, dumpy-muzzled dog, and the presumed personal attractions of its owner."

Foremost among the artists of the day was William Hogarth, a stalwart fancier of the breed, and his inseparable companion was his pug-dog, Trump, whom

[1] "The judges made a display of their knowledge of pugs by sending Roderick out of the ring, disqualifying him for 'carrying his tail on the wrong side'" (Dr. Cryer).

he has immortalised in a painting, which now hangs in the Tate Gallery, of himself and his dog. On its first exhibition it elicited a satire on the two

"Insep'rate companions! and, therefore, you see,
Cheek by jowl they are drawn in familiar degree."

This famous portrait, executed in 1749, was, according to Frederick W. Peel in his *Hogarth and His House*, at first hung in the National Gallery.

Some of Hogarth's other drawings gave offence, and he was himself subject to the venom of his fellow-caricaturists. He was given the name of "Painter Pugg," and in two prints issued in 1753 and 1754 he is depicted with the lower half of his figure being in the form of a pug-dog, whilst one of these prints contains a representation of a pug-dog at the top of the picture.

"The word of professional scoffers and virtuosi,"

writes Austin Dobson, in his *William Hogarth*, published in 1902:

"fell joyously upon its obscurities and incoherencies while the caricaturists diverted themselves hugely with fancy representations of 'Painter Pugg.'"

"Dunce connoisseurs extol the author Pug,
The senseless, tasteless, impudent hum-bug."

Roubillac, the sculptor, was a friend of Hogarth, and not only modelled the bust of Hogarth, which is now in the National Portrait Gallery, but also modelled the pug-dog Trump.

These satires upon the breed and its owners did not affect its general popularity, and David Garrick (1716–79) ridiculed the prevailing fashion in his *Lethe*.

Edward C. Ash gives the following amusing advertisement in his chapter on pug-dogs as relating to the breed, and though the dog required is described as a lap-spaniel of uncertain colour, the description leaves no doubt as to Mrs. Smith wanting a pug-dog. The advertisement was inserted in the *Daily Advertiser*, in November 1744:

"An Exceeding small Lap Spaniel. Any one that has (to dispose of) such a one, either dog or bitch, and of any colour or colours, that is very, very small, with a very *short round snub nose*, and good ears.[1]

"If they will bring it to Mrs. Smith, at a coach-maker's over against the Golden Head, in Great Queen Street, near Lincoln's Inn Fields, they may (if approved of) have a very good purchaser. And to prevent any farther trouble: If it is not exceeding *small* and has anything of a longish peaked nose, it will not at all do. And nevertheless, after this advertisement is published no more, If any person should have a little creature, that answers the character of the advertisement, If they will please but to remember the direction, and bring it to Mrs. Smith, the person is not *so* provided, but that such a one will still at any time be, hereafter, purchased."

It makes one wonder what price was charged in those days per line for an advertisement!

The breed always had royal favour during the time of the first two Georges, but it was on the marriage of George III. to Princess Charlotte of Mecklenburg Strelitz on the 8th September 1761, that they reached the height of popularity. Charlotte was a passionate pug-dog lover, and was never without one or more round her, and the love of her husband for the breed has been kept for us by the portrait, which hangs at Hampton Court, of himself with his pug-dog.

Towards the end of the eighteenth century the un-

[1] Short-nosed lap Spaniels were not known in England till the last century.

rest abroad, followed by wars on the Continent, caused a distinct decrease in the demand for pet dogs ; and though George IV. is said to have kept a pug-dog, neither the pug-dog nor any other breed of dogs seems to have been prominent, despite the fact that Professor Gmelin had discovered three new forms of pug-dog—the Alicant,[1] the Artois and the bastard pug-dog, the latter of which he describes :

" Bastard Pug-Dog. *Canis hybridus.* Has small, half pendulous ears, and a thick flatish nose."

Not much of a description, I am afraid. The following are the classifications of pug-dog as set out by him in his *Animal Kingdom,* translated by Robert Kerr, and published in 1792 :

" Pug-dog. *Canis fricator.* The nose is crooked upwards, the ears are pendulous, and the body square built.
" This variety has a resemblance to the bull-dog, but is much smaller and entirely wants his savage ferocity. Of this there are two sub-varieties, viz. :
" (*a*) The Artois dog, of Buffon, produced between the pug-dog and bastard pug-dog.
" (*b*) The Alicant dog, of Buffon, produced between the pug-dog and Spaniel."

It is rather interesting to consider for a moment as to how pet dogs were treated during this century. Great changes in their treatment had taken place since Dame Juliana Berners, Prioress of St. Albans, wrote in the fifteenth century of " smalle ladye's poppees that bere aweye the flees." Dame Juliana, it is interesting to note, was the first British authoress.

[1] " The Andalusian, or Alicant Dog, has the short muzzle of the pug with the long hair of the spaniel " (William Youatt : *The Dog,* 1845).

A description of the life of a lap-dog is very clearly set out in the first work of canine fiction, *The History of Pompey the Little, or The Life and Adventures of a Lap-dog*, by Francis Coventry, and published in 1751. This book ran through many editions and was very popular in its day, Lowndes describing it as " an admirable *jeu d'esprit*." From the frontispiece to my copy (1773, fifth edition) Pompey would appear to be a type of small spaniel, but the adventures of his life would apply equally well to a pug-dog, as his mistress, " Lady Tempest," also kept with him

" an Italian greyhound, a Dutch pug, two black spaniels of King Charles's breed, a harlequin grey-hound, a spotted Dane and a mouse-coloured English bull-dog."

The meeting of these dogs with their new companion, Pompey, which also includes a description of how lap-dogs were fed in those days, is set out as follows :

" They heard their mistress's rap at the door, and were assembled in the dining-room, ready to receive her : but on the appearance of master Pompey, they set up a general bark, perhaps out of envy ; and some of them treated the little stranger with rather more rudeness than was consistent with dogs of their education. However, the lady soon interposed her authority, and commanded silence among them, by ringing a little bell, which she kept by her for that purpose. They all obeyed the signal instantly, and were still in a moment ; upon which she carried little Pompey round, and obliged them all to salute their new acquaintance, at the same time commanding some of them to ask pardon for their unpolite behaviour ; which whether they understood or not, must be left to the reader's determination. She then summoned a servant, and ordered a chicken to be roasted for him ; but hearing that dinner was just ready to be served up, she was pleased to say, he must be contented with what was provided for herself that day, but gave orders to the cook to get ready a chicken to his own share against night.

"Her ladyship now sat down to table, and Pompey was placed at her elbow, where he received many dainty bits from her fair hands, and was caressed by her all dinner-time, with more than usual fondness."

The agreement for mating Pompey with a dog belonging to a Mrs. Racket was entered into by an exchange of the following two letters :

"Dear Tempest,—My favourite little Veny is at present troubled with certain amorous infirmities of nature, and would not be displeased with the addresses of a lover. Be so good therefore to send little Pompey by my servant who brings this note, for I fancy it will make a very pretty breed, and when the lovers have transacted their affairs, he shall be sent home incontinently.—Believe me, dear Tempest, yours affectionately, Racket."

"Dear Racket,—Infirmities of nature we all are subject to, and therefore I have sent master Pompey to wait upon miss Veny, begging the favour of you to return him as soon as his gallantries are over. Consider, my dear, no modern love can, in the nature of things, last above three days, and therefore I hope to see my little friend again very soon.—Your affectionate friend, "Tempest."

Cruelty was rife, and parents, apparently, made no endeavours to prevent their children treating their pets in the most inhuman manner possible.

"To say the truth, he soon began to find himself very unhappily situated in this family ; for wretched are those animals that become the favourites of children. At first indeed he suffered only the barbarity of their kindness, and was persecuted with no other cruelties than what arose from their extravagant love of him ; but when the date of his favour began to expire (and it did not continue long) he was then taught to feel how much severer their hate could be than their fondness. He had indeed, from the first, two or three dreadful presages of what might happen to him ; for he had seen with his own eyes the two kittens, his playfellows, drowned for some misdemeanor they had been guilty of, and the magpye's head chopt off with the greatest passion, for daring to peck a piece of plumb-cake that lay in the window without permission ; which instances of cruelty were sufficient to warn him, if he had any foresight, of what might afterwards happen to himself.

" But he was not long left to entertain himself with conjectures, before he felt in person and in reality the mischievous disposition of these little tyrants. Sometimes they took it into their heads that he was full of fleas, and then he was soused into a tub of water till he was almost dead, in order to kill the vermin that inhabited the hair of his body. At other times he was set on his hinder legs with a book before his eyes, and ordered to read his lesson ; which not being able to perform, they whipped him till he howled, and then chastised him the more for daring to be sensible of pain."

In those days, before the lethal chamber had been invented, the usual method of destroying a dog appears to have been by hanging : " She rang her bell instantly with the greatest fury, and on the appearance of a footman, ordered him" (the dog) "immediately to be hanged."

If one desires a complete view of the life of a lap-dog during the eighteenth century, the book should be read in full, and it well repays the time spent on it ; but it will be sufficient for our purpose if the above extracts give a rough idea of the position in life occupied by a lap-dog at this period in our history.

CHAPTER V

FRANCE AND ITALY

" You'll be thinking of keeping pug-dogs and parrots next."
                                    D. JERROLD, 1851.

NOT only in England did the pug-dog become popular, but abroad, particularly in Holland, France and Italy. He does not appear to have been really popular in Germany till a later date, though there are traces of him during the eighteenth century in that country.

It is possible that his popularity in Italy started through the introduction of " Punchinello," from the Levant, by Silvio Forillo, about the beginning of the seventeenth century, at Naples ; and the most suitable dog found for the part of Toby was generally a pug-dog—not a poodle, which one would have expected, as poodles were up to that time believed to be the most intelligent dogs for stage work. Probably the pug-dog, on his introduction, appeared the more comical of the two. Certainly, when " Punchinello " reached this country, under the name of " Punch and Judy," during the reign of William III., the part of Toby was always taken by a pug-dog.

Charles Dickens, in his *Shy Neighbours*, mentions two such Tobys :

" I never saw either guilty of the falsehood of failing to look down at the man inside the show, during the whole performance. The difficulty other dogs have in satisfying their minds about these dogs, appears to be never overcome by time. The same dogs must encounter them over and over again as they trudge along in their off minutes behind the legs, and beside the drum, but all dogs seem to suspect their frills and jackets."

But he could never be taken as a lover of the breed; probably he never possessed one. His description of the pug-dog was almost as terrible as that of Washington Irving. I give the description by Dickens from Miss Estelle Ross :

" The novelist tells us that one of his earliest recollections was of a pug-dog, which he met daily on his way to school. It was puffy, ' black-muzzled, with white teeth and crisp curling tail, with a rooted animosity to little boys, barking at them and snapping at their bare legs. . . . From an otherwise unaccountable association of him with a fiddle, we concluded that he was of French extraction and his name Fidèle. He belonged to some female, chiefly inhabiting a back parlour, whose life appears to have been consumed in sniffing and wearing a black beaver bonnet.' "

Washington Irving's description is even worse :

" A little, old, grey-muzzled curmudgeon, with an unhappy eye, that kindles like a coal, if you only look at him ; his nose turns up, his mouth is drawn into wrinkles so as to show his teeth ; in short, he has altogether the look of a dog far gone in misanthropy, and totally sick of the world. When he walks, he has his tail curled up so tight, that it seems to lift his feet from the ground. This wretch is called Beauty."

But we are getting away from the Continent towards the United States, and we will return to Italy with Mrs. Hester Piozzi on her tour of that country in 1786 :

" A transplanted Hollander, carried thither originally from China, seems to thrive particularly well in this part of the world ; the little pug-dog, or Dutch mastiff, which our English ladies were once so fond of, that poor Garrick thought it worth his while to ridicule them for it in the famous dramatic satire called 'Lethe,' has quitted London for Padua, I perceive ; where he is restored happily to his former honours, and every carriage I meet has a *pug* in it. That breed of dogs is now so near expirated among us, that I recollect only Lord Penryn who possesses such an animal."

She found that pug-dogs, as well as other small breeds, were treated with an exaggerated kindness and consideration in Italy.

" A very veracious man "

informed her, she writes,

" yester morning, that his poor wife was half broken-hearted at hearing such a Countess's dog was run over ; 'for,' said he, 'having suckled the pretty creature herself, she loved it like one of her children.' I bid him repeat the circumstance, that no mistake might be made ; he did so ; but seeing me look shocked, or ashamed, or something he did not like, ' Why, Madam,' said the fellow, ' it is a common thing enough for ordinary men's wives to suckle the lap-dogs of ladies of quality ' ; adding that they were paid for their milk, and he saw no harm in gratifying one's *superiors*. As I was disposed to see nothing *but* harm in disputing with such a competitor, our conference finished soon ; but the fact is certain."

Thomas Bewick (1753-1828), in his *History of Quadrupeds*, also bears out the affection of the Ladies of Italy for the pug-dog and claims that

" it still maintains its place in the favour of the fair ones of that country."

Buffon shows clearly the popularity of the pug-dog in France at his day and he gives two names to the breed, which he calls *Le Doguin ou Mopse*. These two names are rather curious. "Le Doguin" approximately means the small *dogue* (bull-dog), and "Mopse" being a derivation, I presume, of the German name for the breed, *Mopshund*.

Idstone, dealing with this question of foreign names, states :

"That their jet-black muzzle obtained for them the name of *carlins*, from the famous Parisian Harlequin, but they were previously known as *Doguins*, or *Roquets*, though now they are known as Pugs in France and Italy. The name Carlin is interesting, as proving that the black mask was valued in France ; though it was either overlooked, or they did not take the trouble to attain it, in Italy."

As a matter of fact, *Carlin* is the common name for the breed at the present day in France, and the name given to it in Italy is *Cagnuolo*.[1]

But perhaps the greatest of pug-dog lovers of all time was to be found in France. This was Madame Josephine Beauhaernais, who was never without one, even during the days of her imprisonment. During the French Revolution she was imprisoned in the Carmelite monastery of Les Carmes—in the same cell, as a matter of interest, with Madame Tussaud, the originator of the wax-work exhibition near Baker Street. She later married the great Napoleon.

I do not think I can do better to describe her love for the breed than give two extracts, the first from Miss Estelle Ross's *Book of Noble Dogs*, and the second from *Josephine, Empress and Queen*, written by Frédéric Masson in 1899 :

"Napoleon was not personally attached to dogs, though Josephine's little Fortuné, who came into her

[1] Other Italian names are : *scimmiotto* (little monkey) and *fanciullino* (little child).

possession when she was living at Carmes,[1] was used as a messenger between his mistress and Bonaparte, carrying little missives under his collar. He was no beauty, a bit of a mongrel, long in the body, low in the leg, russet-coloured, with the black muzzle and curly tail of a pug.

" Josephine's fondness for Fortuné nearly led to a quarrel with Napoleon on their wedding-night. Levy, in *La Vie Intime*, recalls a conversation which the general had with Arnault. Pointing to Josephine's dog lying on the sofa, he said :

" ' Do you see that gentleman : he is my rival. He was in possession of Madame's bed when I married her. I wished to remove him : it was quite useless to think of it. I was told that I must either sleep elsewhere or consent to share my bed. That annoyed me considerably, but I had to make up my mind. I gave way. The favourite was less accommodating. I bear proofs on my legs of what I say.'

" The general bore no grudge, for a few months later he wrote to his consort sending a ' million kisses even to Fortuné, notwithstanding his naughtiness.'

" The favourite met a cruel fate in being killed by the cook's bull-dog,[2] and Napoleon hoped and intended

[1] According to Philip W. Sergeant, in his *Empress Josephine, Napoleon's Enchantress*, Fortuné belonged to her before her imprisonment, and was introduced into the prison as a bearer of secret messages, which he carried under his collar.

[2] The grief at the loss of Fortuné is described by Philip W. Sergeant as follows :

" Only one blow seems to have come to lessen her happiness—the death of Fortuné. This little pug-dog, whom Napoleon once told Arnault that he found in possession of Madame's bed when he married, and who showed his resentment at the intruder by taking a piece out of his leg, did not limit his hostility to men. He met the cook's dog in the garden at Montebello, and treating him like Napoleon, found him far from equally complacent. The result was that Fortuné was discovered dead. ' It is a most tragic death,' writes Arnault. ' I leave you to imagine what was his Mistress's grief. The Conqueror of Italy could not but show his sympathy. He mourned sincerely for an accident which left him sole possessor of his wife's bed.' But Josephine consoled herself. She that it would be the last of the Empress's favourites, but she promptly provided a pug-dog as his successor—as she was exceptionally fond of this breed. The Emperor, in protest, interviewed the bull-dog assassin and suggested to him that he should devour the pug !

" The newcomer was very regular in his habits. As the lady of the bedchamber left the Empress for the night he followed her to her room—Napoleon had had his way as to another canine bedfellow—sleeping quietly on a chair by her bedside. In the morning, with his tail tightly curled, he waited in the ante-chamber till Josephine's door opened, which was his signal to rush in and overwhelm her with affectionate greeting."

Masson gives a long description of Josephine's dogs which, as will be seen from the following extract, were not always pug-dogs.

" The door is opened to admit the favourite dog, for none but Fortuné had had the privilege of sleeping in his mistress's room and disputing the entrée with Napoleon. Ugly as he was, however, short-legged, long-bodied, not so much tawny as red, with a nose like a weasel, and nothing but the face and the corkscrew-tail to proclaim him a pug, Fortuné had belonged to Josephine in 1793, and, when the Carmelite Monastery was her prison, the notes of warning or of safety were hidden underneath his collar. Fortuné was gone ; he had been strangled at Mombello by the cook's big dog. Josephine then adopted a female pet, and so much attached was she to the little animal that she sent for Moscati, the most celebrated physician in Milan, to attend it in an illness. This brought Moscati under Napoleon's notice and made his fortune. He became President of the Cisalpine Directory, deputy to the Council of Lyons, Director-General of Public Instruction, Count, Great Dignitary of the Iron Crown and senator of the kingdom, because he had not scorned

' did as many a woman does to comfort herself for the loss of a lover ; she took another.' And Fortuné never lacked a successor during the lifetime of Josephine."

such a patient. The little lap-dog's successor, a pug, had a place assigned to it in the carriage next after that of the Empress from the time of the Dieppe ' voyage ' in the year XI. The pug was a personage well acquainted with etiquette, and never failed, when the dresser retired after the Empress was in bed, to follow her, whomsoever she might be, into her room, where he turned himself round on a chair, and there remained until morning. Then he would go down in a leisurely manner to the ' Salon d'annonce ' and wait patiently until the door of his mistress's room was opened, when he would rush in with an air of wild delight and the liveliest demonstrations of affection. A brack-hound of the smallest species, given by M. de Colbert, failed, notwithstanding his hunting talents, to dethrone the pug, or rather the pugs, for there was a family of them. . . . These dogs had their own special ' bonne ' (her name was La Brisée), and their keep in ordinary years varied from 350 to 450 fr., but in 1806 rose to 568 francs : they were with the Empress the whole day, lay close to her on the sofa, where she made a cushion for them of her ' cachemire,' announced visitors as well as the chamberlains and ushers, attacked everybody who approached their mistress, had a special liking for the red calves of Cardinals' legs, and would tear the robe that displeased them to rags, without any respect for its lining.''

CHAPTER VI

ENGLAND DURING THE NINETEENTH CENTURY

> " A Pug did not suit me at all ;
> The feature unluckily rose up,
> And folks took offence
> When offering pence
> Because of his turning his nose up."
>   G. T. Hood : " Lament of a Poor Blind."

WE have now reached the great century in canine history. Many new breeds came into being and a much greater interest altogether was taken in the canine race.

So far as pugdom was concerned the greatest civil war that was ever known in dogdom was fought, concluding, rather like the Wars of the Roses, in the junction between the two houses of Morrison and Willoughby. Unfortunately, although the war was waged so recently, it is extremely difficult to give accurate dates. All the established facts were shattered by the Mayhew letter, and it seems certain that a mistake of, at least, a matter of twenty years has been made somewhere with respect to the Willoughby strain. But of this more anon.

The century opened badly so far as dogs were concerned. The whole country was agitated with internal industrial strife, and the threatened Napoleonic invasion kept everybody in a state of high nervous tension. People in those days did not realise that the famous Napoleonic star was a " dog star," and the divorce of Josephine and the separation from the influence of her pug-dogs was the moment from which Napoleon's fortunes waned, and Elba and St. Helena were to follow.

Not only was no breed of dogs popular at the beginning of the century, but it opened with a distinct and definite attack on the pug-dog.

The author of *The Sportsman's Cabinet*, published in 1804, threw down the gauntlet which, unfortunately, was not taken up till many years afterwards.

" It is clear that the pug-dog, from its singularity, affords more doubt in the certainty of its origin than almost any of the species. It is asserted by some, that the genuine breed was introduced to this island from Muscovy, and that they were, originally, the undoubted natives of that country ; others assert the pug to have been produced by a commixture between the English bull-dog and the little Dane, calling such races single mongrels, as coming from the mixture of two pure races ; but there are other dogs which may, with propriety, be called double mongrels, because they come from a mixture of a pure race, and of one already mixed. The shock-dog, for instance, is a double mongrel, as being produced by the pug and the small Dane. The dog of Alicant is also a double mongrel, as coming from the whelp and small spaniel ; and the Maltese, or lap-dog, is a double mongrel produced by the small spaniel with the barbet ; the spaniel and the little dane produce the lion-dog,[1] which is very scarce. . . .

" For, perhaps, in the whole catalogue of the canine-species, there is not one of less utility, or possessing less the powers of attraction than the pug-dog, applicable to no sport, appropriated to no useful purpose, susceptible of no predominant passion, and in no way whatever remarkable for any extra eminence, he is continued from era to era for what alone he might have

[1] Maltese were known as " the lion-dog," but he has mentioned this. Possibly he means the Pekin spaniel.

4

been originally intended, the patient follower of a ruminating philosopher, or the adulating and consolatory companion of an old maid."

This statement, upon which comment is superfluous, was not criticised till Hugh Dalziel, in 1888, said that the writer of the above quotation was

" a cantankerous old bachelor, caring for nothing but his pipe, his pointer, and his gun " ;

and Rawdon B. Lee, commenting on the quotation in 1894, writes :

" The above is rather rough on the poor little pug, but such an unfair and ungallant description could only have emanated from the brain of a rough sportsman of the old school, whose chief delights would lay in badger drawing, bull baiting and cock fighting. The pug-dog has its uses in society, and possesses credentials as a lady's dog that cannot be excelled."

However, the description given in *The Sportsman's Cabinet* was accepted and did the breed great harm— much more, in fact, than the petty writers on canine matters who believed it to be amusing to vilify the breed during its popularity in the mid-Victorian era. One is glad, however, to be able to state that no writer on canine matters, whose works have been successful enough to be generally accepted and quoted at the present day, has criticised the pug-dog unfairly.

The writers on the subject, omitting writers on natural history, pure and simple, who have stood the test of time may be taken to be Idstone, G. R. Jesse, Stonehenge (J. W. Walsh), H. Dalziel, Rawdon B. Lee and, of a later day. W. D. Drury, Robert Leighton, James Watson and Edward C. Ash. Sometimes their criticisms may seem unkind, but they can be taken as none the less honest.

One rather amusing incident may be mentioned. Pug-dogs were given two new names at the beginning of the century, and these seem to have held to the breed for a considerable time : they were " the figure-of-eight dog " and " the jug-handled dog." The former name was, I take it, given to them because of their appearance either with regard to the tightly curled tail, or—which is even more likely—referring to the pug-dog's peculiar and characteristic walk when advancing towards any one, especially when he entertains pleasurable anticipations such as reciprocated affection, namely, a wriggling motion from side to side describing the semi-circular shape of the figure-of-eight ; and the latter name has been explained by T. W. Knox in his *Dog Stories and Dog Lore*, published in 1887 :

" ' Yes,' replied Mr. Graham, ' and this peculiar curve of the tail has given the pug the name of Jug-handled Dog.'
" ' How is that ? '
" ' Why, there's been a joke going the rounds of the papers that an enterprising dog-dealer had taken advantage of this peculiarity of the pug to make a handle by which he could be carried ; by cutting a hole in the animal's skin, along his back, and grafting the tail into it until it became firm and the sore healed, it was asserted that a handle was formed by which the dog could be carried on a lady's arm like a workbag or hand-satchel, picked up to be transported over street crossings, or hung up on a nail or peg whenever desired.' There have been many absurd stories told about the pug, but this is the worst of all."

The reason for the great interest shown during the latter half of the nineteenth century in canine matters was due to a small spark struck at Newcastle-upon-Tyne in June 1859, when a gun-maker called Pape, whose shop is still extant in Collingwood Street of that

city, offered a prize of some guns to the owner of the
best pointer shown.   Sixty dogs entered, and it was said
that such a collection of dogs had never before been
seen together.   The excitement created by this show
was immense, and dog shows were held in the same year
at Birmingham and Edinburgh.   Not only was England
seized with the new sport of showing dogs, but even the
Continent took up the game, and a show was held in
Paris in 1865.   Edward C. Ash, writing on the subject
of these early shows, states :

" In the early show days of Birmingham (1860), the
first show in which non-sporting dogs were catered for,
was a class for pugs, but there appear to have been no
entries.   Leeds (1861) also had a class in which a first
and second prize were awarded, but not the third.   At
the 1861 Manchester Show the prize-winner is given :
' 1st, the Female Blondin.' "

The popular enthusiasm for these shows led to the
founding, by a Mr. S. E. Sherley, of a club for dogs in
April 1873, so that shows might be regulated and the
points of the various breeds defined.

The founding of this club, The Kennel Club, led to
the formation of various clubs for special breeds, and
The Pug Dog Club,[1] was early in the field.   The first
of the four British pug-dog clubs [2] which have been in
existence, and which still retains its place at the present
day, was founded in 1882, within ten years of the founda-
tion of " The Kennel Club."

The first Kennel Club Stud Book shows an entry of

[1] The present Hon. Secretary is Miss E. D. Gilpin, The Hague,
Hanworth Road, Hounslow.

[2] The Pug-Dog Club, The London and Provincial Pug Club
(now amalgamated with The Pug-Dog Club), The Northern
Pug Club, which is still in existence, and The Scottish Pug-Dog
Club.

sixty-six pug-dogs, and amongst the pedigrees is given that of Cloudy, who will be mentioned hereafter :

"Cloudy, 3756, bred by Lady Churston, by Mayhew's Click, out of Topsy ; Click by Lamb (from Pekin) out of Moss."

Queen Victoria had a real love for dogs, but her chief affection was for her little dog Dash, a spaniel, and Waldman, a dachshund, whose grave is inscribed at Windsor : " The very favourite dachshund of Queen Victoria, who brought him from Baden, 1872 ; died, July 11, 1881."

Dash belonged to her mother, as the following extract from her diary, published by Viscount Esher, in 1912, under the title of *The Girlhood of Queen Victoria*, for the year 1833, will show :

" *Tuesday, 15th January.*—I awoke at 7 and got up at 8. At 10 minutes to 9 we breakfasted. At half-past 9 came the Dean till half-past 11. Just before we went out, Mamma's little dog, a beautiful spaniel of King Charles's breed, called Dash, and which Sir John gave her yesterday, came and will now remain here."

She was so fond of this little dog that, after her coronation, C. P. R. Leslie tells us in his *Recollections* that :

" When the state coach drove up to the steps of the palace, she heard the spaniel barking with joy in the hall, and exclaimed, ' There's Dash ! ' and was in a hurry to lay aside the sceptre and ball she carried in her hands, and take off the crown and robes *to go and wash little Dash*."

But despite her love for Dash and Waldman and her other dogs, the Queen kept a fawn pug-dog in later years, but I cannot trace this dog's name ; and she certainly had a terrible black creature with cropped ears and a white chest and feet, called a black pug-dog, in her kennels in 1854.

Pug-dogs were, as we have seen, extremely scarce at the beginning of the nineteenth century, and the earliest established breeder would appear to have been an innkeeper of Walham Green called Charles (or, more commonly, Charlie) Morrison, who bred the usual Dutch type of pug-dogs in a very small way about 1840. The Dutch type may be taken shortly to be, in comparison with present-day pug-dogs, light, clear, golden fawn, short nosed, with little wrinkle, massive in size, with a clearly defined, but thin, trace and thumb mark.

He was easily superseded by the more vigorous and pushful breeder, Mrs. Laura Mayhew, who commenced with the same type of dogs, but later introduced specimens imported from China. Other breeders of the day, in a minor way, were Mr. H. Gilbert and Mr. W. Macdonald, both of London. As Stonehenge says, the pug-dog

"was exceedingly rare in the middle of the present" (nineteenth) "century, even a moderately good one not being procurable for less than £30, and that at a time when £5 was the average price of a lady's pet, even of the fashionable kinds."

Now, the efforts of Mrs. Mayhew excited Charlie Morrison to extend his breeding, and the introduction of Chinese blood into her strain gave his dogs a personality of their own which came to be known as "The Morrison Strain" or, more simply, "Morrison's." These efforts on the parts of the breeders started the pug-dog on his road to favour.

The Morrison strain is very important, so I will quote at length from Stonehenge, who was a friend of his:

"According to Mr. Morrison's statement to me (which, however, he did not wish made public during his life), this strain was lineally descended from a stock possessed by Queen Charlotte, one of which is painted with great care in the well-known portrait of George III. at Hampton Court ; but I could never get him to reveal the exact source from which it was obtained. That he himself fully believed in the truth of this story I am quite confident ; and I am also of opinion that he never hazarded a statement of which he had the slightest doubt—being in this respect far above the average of 'doggy' men. Although he never broadly stated as much, I always inferred that the breed was obtained by 'back-stair influence,' and on that account a certain amount of reticence was necessary ; but, whatever may be the cause of the secrecy maintained, I fully believe the explanation given by Mr. Morrison of the origin of this breed of pugs, which is as commonly known by his name as that of Lady Willoughby de Eresby by hers. His appeal to the Hampton Court portrait, in proof of the purity of his breed from its general resemblance to the dog in that painting, goes for nothing in my mind, because you may breed up to any type by careful selection ; but I do not hesitate to endorse his statement as to the Guelph origin of his strain, because I have full confidence in his truthfulness, from having tested it in various other ways. I need scarcely remark that both strains are derived from the Dutch—'the Morrison' coming down to us through the three Georges from William III., and 'the Willoughby' being a more recent importation direct from Holland and Vienna. Both strains are equally lively in temperament, moderately tricky and companionable, but their chief advantage as pets is that they are unusually free from smell both in breath and coat."

Now let us read what Stonehenge has to say with regard to the great rival of the Morrison strain, which afterwards got the name of the " Willoughby " strain.

" During the decade 1840–50, however, several admirers of pugs attempted to breed them from good foreign strains. Foremost among these was the then

Lady Willoughby de Eresby, who after a great deal of trouble obtained a dog from Vienna which had belonged to a Hungarian countess, but was of a bad colour, being a mixture of the stone fawn now peculiar to the ' Willoughby strain,' and black ; but the combination of these colours was to a certain extent in the brindled form. From accounts which are to be relied on, this dog was about twelve inches high, and of good shape, both in body and head, but with a face much longer than would now be approved of by pug-fanciers. In 1846 he was mated with a fawn bitch imported from Holland, of the desired colour, viz., stone fawn in body, with black mask and trace, but with no indication of brindle. She had a shorter face and heavier jowl than the dog, and was altogether in accordance with the type now recognised as the correct ' Willoughby pug.' From this pair are descended all the strain named after Lady Willoughby de Eresby, which are marked in colour by their peculiar cold stone fawn, and the excess of black often showing itself, not in brindled stripes, but in entirely or nearly entirely black heads, and large ' saddle marks ' or wide ' traces.' "

The points to be noted particularly in this statement by Stonehenge are the date at which Lady Willoughby commenced breeding and the origin of her strain. This is important, as it is the evidence of a contemporary writer, and other writers have followed him. So far as the Morrison strain is concerned I think we can accept Stonehenge, but I am going to suggest, for your consideration, that he was entirely wrong with regard to the Willoughby strain.

It will be noted that Stonehenge certainly makes no reference to the Mayhew strain, except stating that Mrs. Mayhew was an exhibitor " of late years," and if it would not be sacrilege to suggest it in connection with such an established authority, I cannot help suspecting that he has mixed up the early Mayhew strain with that of the Willoughby—though, again, I can trace nothing authoritative, except the statement of Stonehenge, with regard to the pug-dog imported from Vienna. However, Stonehenge's statement is important and must be given its full value.

Now let us consider the following letter from Reginald E. Mayhew of New York, son of Mrs. Laura Mayhew, which is published by James Watson in *The Dog Book* :

" When shows were first promoted in England it was generally accepted that pugs had been imported to that country from Holland, Russia and China. How near or how wide of the mark were those responsible for this I will leave to others. I do know, however, that this was the opinion harboured by such authorities as Lord Willoughby D'Eresby, Charlie Morrison, Mr. Rawlins, Mr. Bishop and my mother.

" At the outset the winning English pugs were of Dutch origin, and among the chief breeders were my mother and Mr. Morrison, the latter being landlord of an old-fashioned roadhouse, in the outskirts of Chelsea.

" In those days pugs were cropped, and in general type were tight-skinned, straight-faced, apricot fawn in colour, and as a rule had good, wide-set eyes, which gave them a fairly good expression.

" A few years afterwards—in the later 'sixties—Lord Willoughby became a prominent factor in pugdom, so much so that the term Willoughby pug was as common an expression in the breed as Laverack setter in English setters. Lord Willoughby, who lived near us at Twickenham, obtained his original specimens from a tight-rope walker known as the female Blondin, who brought them from St. Petersburg. They were silver fawns, the majority being smutty in colour, with pinched faces and small eyes, but better wrinkled than the Dutchmen.

" Reverting to their colour, I have seen so many born practically black in those old days, and consigned to the bucket on that account, that I have often marvelled that more recent exhibitors should have been so deluded as to consider the introduction of the black pugs a novelty. In fact, when Lady Brassey introduced the black variety her specimens had the inherent faults of the Willoughby strain—pinched faces, small eyes and legginess—plus tight skins. And so it is to-day, to a less marked degree, in specimens of this shading. In fact, the only really good-headed black I have seen here was Mrs. Howard Gould's Black Knight.

" With the advent of the smutty coloured Russians, breeders mingled their blood with that of the Hollanders, with the result that faces—through Rawlin's Crusoe, a good headed Dutchman—and Mr. Bishop's Pompey— bred half Dutch and half Russian—showed a slight improvement, while colour and shadings were a distinct advancement.

" Still, the winning specimens, typical as they were, lacked that grandeur in head which the ideal called for. Nor was it until my mother became the owner of Click that really grand heads and beautiful expressions were seen on the bench. Click has long been a household name in pugdom, as for more than twenty-five years the crack winners have traced back to him. In fact, all the great skulls, big, appealing eyes, square muzzles and short faces are due to Click. Chiefly through his daughter Cloudy—which was also owned by my mother —and in a minor degree through his union with Gipsey, a long-faced, undershot creature, belonging to Mrs. Lee, of Toy Spaniel fame, has his name become so closely associated with champions.

" Gipsey had three litters, containing specimens worthy of the highest praise. Unfortunately, however, Mrs. Lee, besides dogs, had in her cramped quarters a pet monkey, which, in spite of his owner's vigilance, succeeded in either killing the offspring or mutilating them. One of these was Odin, whose name is to be found in many pedigrees. In his case, the monkey had bitten off his tail to such effect that hardly any vestige of it was left.

" As to Click himself, he was an apricot fawn, with an ideal head and expression and most beautiful eyes. He was, on the leg, rather narrow behind, and as rough in coat as Mrs. Gould's Black Knight. In fact, alter the latter's colour and one would have a very good example of Click.

" Click's parents—Lamb and Moss—were Chinese beyond dispute. They were captured in the Emperor of China's palace during the siege of Pekin in 1867 or 1868, and were brought to England by the then Marquis of Wellesley, I think. Anyhow, they were given to a Mrs. St. John, who brought them several times to our house. Alike as two peas, they were solid apricot fawn, without a suspicion of white ; had lovely heads and expressions ; but, unlike their son, they were close to the ground, and a shade long in body. The pair were so much alike that my mother was firmly of the opinion they were brother and sister.

" I have purposely referred to the colour of Lamb and Moss, because when Click became a success as a sire, the story was circulated that his parents were lemon and white Japanese spaniels, and as few breeders had seen either Lamb or Moss the rumour was generally accepted.

" With the advent of Tragedy and his son Comedy,[1] the era of heads began. Both were colossal in stature, Tragedy being a dog in Scarborough so huge that he was called Tichborne, after the claimant. His (Tragedy's) dam, Judy, was by Click and from Mrs. Lee's Gipsey, while Comedy was by Tragedy from Cloudy, who, by the by, was an exceptionally good bitch, and should never have been beaten in the ring.

" I should say the best pugs I have seen are Miss Jacquet's Tum Tum, Mr. Booth's Comedy, Mrs. Foster's Jennie, Mrs. Britain's Little Count and Little Countess, Mrs. Maule's Little Duke, Miss Houldsworth's Dowager and Countess, and my mother's Hebe.

" I cannot leave the pug subject without expressing regret that popular feeling tends to hold the breed in a contemptuous cum ridiculous light. No breed in its specimens has such distinct individuality. In character the pug is brimful of intelligence ; it is consequential to a degree ; is willing to take its own part ; does not

[1] Belonging to Mr. Foster, and winner of the first prize at Birmingham in 1877.

possess an atom of shyness, and in the old days—when I was in swaddling clothes—and my parents lived in Derbyshire, the men used to take Tootie and her sons and daughters out ratting with ferrets. Being close and short-coated, pugs do not require half the attention called for by the more popular variety of toys, such as Pomeranians, Spaniels and Yorkshire terriers, while they are more robust in constitution and of a more independent spirit."

Commenting on this very interesting letter, James Watson writes :

"The information as to the Willoughby pugs is entirely new so far as we had any knowledge, and it rather dissipates the prevailing impression that certainly existed thirty years ago that the Willoughby pugs were an old and well-established strain. We recall the name of the female Blondin, but nothing as to the date she was performing in England. Blondin, after whom she was named, was there in 1858, so that if we say the Willoughby pugs date back to 1860, that will be near enough. This is borne out by what the stud book shows as to the introduction of the Willoughby blood into outside channels, for that appears to have first taken place about 1867, though one or two older dogs are said to have been of Lord Willoughby's strain. When it comes down to names, however, this seems to be the oldest pedigree we have : 'Mungo, born 1868, bred by Lord Willoughby, by his Ruby out of his Cora, out of his Mina. Ruby by Romeo out of Romah, out of Lady Shaftesbury's Cassy.' This is a peculiar pedigree, but even as it stands it is the exceptionally long one in the first volume of the stud book, which was anything but errorless as to names, breeding or reference numbers. The pedigree of Cloudy, the great brood bitch Mr. Mayhew refers to, is given as by Click out of Topsy, by Lamb out of Moss, whereas that is the Click extension.
"Mr. Morrison was as old a breeder as Mrs. Mayhew, probably older, and as his hostelry was a house of call

for many persons, his pugs became well known. Outside of these West End of London breeders, there were many throughout England who owned, exhibited and bred pugs, but pedigree was very little thought of and very few pugs were equipped with one. We may take it, however, that the very great majority of the pugs, prior to the Willoughby and the Pekin introductions, were descendants of the Dutch pugs, or of pugs which came from China some time during the seventeenth century."

I would like to remind readers of the name of the winner of the Manchester Show of 1861, and to add that the Stud Book gives Click to be " by Lamb (from Pekin) out of Moss," and also mention that Leatherhead (George Lowe), in one of his *Pillars of the Stud-Book*, stated that Moss was said to be a Willoughby pug-dog.

This is all very confusing, I will admit, and it is one of my hopes that the publication of this book will bring forth information which will help the mystery to be cleared up as to how and when the Willoughby strain first started.

One is glad to be able to state, that however furious the fight was while it lasted between the adherents to the Willoughbys and the Morrisons, the battle was amicably settled by the interbreeding of the two strains, which proves that the League of Nations may do some good after all !

The Pug-Dog Club was founded, as we have seen, in 1882, by the efforts of Mr. T. Proctor ; but it was not until 1887 that the points of the breed were settled, chiefly on those given by Stonehenge. The London and Provincial Pug Club was formed soon afterwards, and a separate standard of points, which were never adhered to, were drawn up by that society. Shows by the Pug-Dog Club are now held annually. There is a good description in *The Stock Keeper* of the 19th of June 1885 of the club show for that year, which proves that the club had held earlier shows and has probably held an annual show ever since its commencement:

"The Pug Club Show at the Aquarium has surpassed all similar undertakings in respect to gate-money. There is no mistake about pugs being first favourites with the fair sex. The gallery was full of ladies.

"Several of the winners wore necklaces. Miss Rennie's Lion (first prize) was bedecked with a chaplet of turquoise beads, which were a source of much annoyance to the poor little chap, who kept catching his paws in the strings. This is exemplifying the French saying, ' Il faut souffrir pour être beau.'

"The Pug Club had engaged the same show-man, whose vociferous efforts were equal to the occasion.

"'Now then! Now then! Now then!!! This way for the Puggery. Come and see puggie, puggie, puggie!'"

It was by no means unusual for pug-dogs to wear valuable jewellery, and the pug-dogs belonging to the late Lord Anglesey were always bejewelled and expensively turned out.

Another reference to the breed in the same paper, *The Stock Keeper*, for April 1885, contains another peculiar announcement with regard to pug-dogs:

" PUG FRIGHTENED TO DEATH

" One of the entries at the Central Hall was that of the pug Lady Rosebud, but the bitch was absent, having died from fright caused by being chased by another of her owner's pugs which was tied to a basket. The dog dragged this basket along, and so frightened Lady Rosebud and another, Prince Edward, that both died. The owner, Captain C. R. Harris, last year lost a pug under very similar circumstances. It was frightened to death by a tramp looking into the room through a window."

There can be no question that in the 'eighties the pug-dog was at the height of its popularity not only in this country but all over Europe; doubtless it nearly reached the height as that to which it will ascend in the present century. Hugh Dalziel, writing in 1888, states :

"As soon as the tide of fashion turned and again set in for pugs, the creation of the supply commenced, and now, like so many others, the Pug market is overstocked, and everywhere, in town and country, these animals swarm. . . . Dogs of Pug character are widely distributed : a dog nearly akin to him is met with in China and Japan, he is well known in Russia, a favourite in Germany, plentiful in Holland and Belgium and common enough in France."

The chief publications of the nineteenth century on the most part were appreciative—J. C. Wood, in 1851, describing him as

"A cheerful and amusing companion, and very affectionate in disposition. Sometimes it is apt to be rather snappish to strangers, but this is a fault which is common to all lap-dogs which are not kept in proper order by their possessors. For those who cannot spend much time in the open-air it is a more suitable companion than any other dog, because it can bear the confinement of the house better than any other of the canine species ; and, indeed, seems to be as much at home on a carpet as is a canary on the perch of its cage. Moreover, it is almost wholly free from the unpleasant odour with which the canine race is affected."

Idstone, in 1872, writes :

"I have seldom if ever seen a Pug-dog shy, snappish, or sulky ; generally they are ready to be friendly with strangers—unexcitable and indifferent. Cleanliness is their chief attraction, and a certain high-bred demeanour. . . . I cannot say that I am an admirer of their form . . . but their colour—exactly that of a mastiff—is, to my mind, exquisite."

And Rawdon B. Lee can be taken to sum up the evidence produced during the century when he wrote in 1894 :

"As a companion in the house, and for an occasional run into the country, no dog is better fitted than the pug. He is cleanly in his habits, has a pretty, soft coat, and nice skin ; no foul smell hangs about him, and he is gentleness itself. He shows no ill-temper or mopishness, and the objectionable lolling out of the tongue and unpleasant snorting, which at one time were so common in this variety, is quickly disappearing. Of several pugs that I have owned or known, not more than one of them was addicted to either of these unpleasant habits. All were lively and tractable, and if not actually as intelligent as a highly trained poodle, one pug I knew was quite accomplished in many little tricks he used to perform. No doubt had a professional trainer taken this little dog in hand, it would have been able to earn more than its own living on the stage. Again, a pug can remain sweet and healthy on less open-air exercise than any other dog, and two of them will play about the dining-room or nursery and amuse themselves as much as two terriers would by a scamper in the open fields.

"The pug is not a hunting dog, except as far as tracking the footsteps of his fair mistress is concerned, but he has been known to take to the unladylike occupation of killing rats, which he has done as well as a terrier. Still, it is no part of the duties of a lady's lap-dog to soil his pretty mouth by contact with the most obnoxious of creatures, because we all know that perhaps the next minute he may be fondled and caressed by his owner.

"Although I have said a pug-dog can do with comparatively little outdoor exercise, still, he is better for as much as he can be given, for no dog has a greater tendency to put on fat, and reach a state of obesity, than the one of which I write. Whoever saw a pug-dog thin and gaunt, with its ribs and backbone almost sticking through the skin ? He always looks smooth, contented, and comfortable, eats well, and he should have as little meat and fat-producing food as possible. Some writers have given him the reputation of stupidity, but I do not believe him deserving of such an epithet.   In the house and out of doors he is as sensible as any other dog, follows well in a crowd when properly trained, and is no more liable to lose himself than an ordinary terrier. Some friends of mine had what they called a pug, but she was not more than half or three-parts pure bred, who was particularly sensible.   She would retrieve, kill rats, was fond of the gun, and liked a ride on the 'bus or tramcar so well that she continually would take one on her own account, which the kindly conductor allowed her to have gratuitously, the conditions of the 'tram' company notwithstanding.   This dog had the curly tail, fawn colour, and general appearance of a pure-bred animal, excepting that she was rather long in face. She lived to a great age, but as a rule the pug is not the longest lived of the canine race."

Towards the end of the century, however, the popularity of the pug-dog waned ; the introduction of shows had brought new breeds into the arena, and novelty was the order of the day.   Foremost among these new breeds, if one can call a dog a new breed which can carry its history back to 200 years B.C.—but a new breed from a popular point of view in this country—was the pomeranian.   For some time the pug-dog kept up its prominence against the enormous numbers of pomeranians, which were being imported from Germany ; but finally the advent of the pekinese drove it from its position of being the most popular toy-dog.   The excitement created by the arrival of the pekinese was phenomenal, and no sooner had breeding started in earnest than all other breeds of toy-dogs were swept before it, and it attained the position it retains to this day of being the premier toy-dog.

Before ending this chapter I should like to mention a few of the outstanding pug-dogs of the nineteenth century.   I have already mentioned the champions of

5

the Mayhew, Morrison and Willoughby strains, but there are still a great many pug-dogs by other breeders who were famous during the late nineteenth and early twentieth century. I do not think I can do better than to give the list set out in *Cassell's New Book of the Dog* :

" Mr. T. Proctor . . . has owned some very good dogs, of which Ch. Confidence was one of the best. Confidence was a very high-class dog, correct in colour and markings, but was a size too big, as also was his son York, another remarkably fine Pug, correct in every other respect, and considered by many to be the most perfect fawn Pug of his day. He was exhibited by Mr. Proctor when a puppy, and purchased at that time by Mrs. Gresham, who now also owns that charming little representative of his breed, Ch. Grindley King, who only weighs 14 lb., and is the perfection of a ladies' pet. Grindley King is one of the few Pugs that have a level mouth, and he is squarer in muzzle than most bigger dogs, whilst few Pugs have as much wrinkle and loose skin. He, however, has his faults, as he might be a little finer in coat, and he has not black toe-nails. The late Mr. W. L. Sheffield, of Birmingham, was an admirer of small Pugs, his Ch. Stingo Sniffles being a beautiful specimen and quite the right size. The late Mr. Maule's Royal Duke reminds one what a fawn Pug should be, and Mrs. Brittain had two famous Pugs, whilst Mr. Mayo's Ch. Earl of Presbury, Mr. Robert's Keely Shrimp, and Mr. Harvey Nixon's Ch. Royal Rip were very grand dogs. Mrs. Benson's Ch. Julius Cæsar has had a successful career ; he was bred by the late Mrs. Dunn, who owned a large kennel of good Pugs ; and Miss Little's Ch. Betty of Pomfret was an excellent one of the right size. Another very beautiful little Pug is Mrs. James Currie's Ch. Sylvia."

To this list of the great ones may, I think, be added not unfairly two pug-dogs who helped to keep the breed in the limelight outside the show-ring—one on the stage, and the other in the courts.

The first is an extract from a newspaper of 1898 :

" This is an amazingly clever pug, belonging to Mr. and Mrs. B. Melville, who are well known in the entertainment world. This little dog takes the part of the ' coon ' baby in a picturesque little stage spectacle. Dressed in baby's costume, she walks about the stage on her hind legs, looking very quaint, as you may imagine. After this sketch she goes through a performance entirely on her own account, merely looking to Mrs. Melville for the cue. This is one of the cleverest dog contortionists in the world. In the accompanying photo [1] we see that the animal has thrown herself into the favourite posture of human contortionists—a kind of reversed S. Mr. Melville will tell you that this little pug has a natural aptitude for performing, which renders a great amount of training quite superfluous."

The other pug-dog I have to mention caused a sensation in a law court, and the account is taken from the *Kennel Gazette* of January 1890 :

" Mr. Hannay recently had a case before him at Marlborough Street which puzzled him completely. Two ladies claimed a pug-dog as their own, and evidence was given by both sides in support of their respective cases. The dog made matters worse, for when one of the disputants called, ' Moppy, Moppy, come along, Moppy,' he evinced as much joy as if his owner was at last found. But when the other party to the suit called, ' Jem,' he went to her, and was equally obliging to any one who called. The magistrate found in this a loophole by which to escape the dilemma, to his evident relief, and he declined to make any order."

---

[1] I regret I have been unable to reproduce the photo of the contortionist, so I hopefully leave its diverting antics to the imagination of the reader.

CHAPTER VII

BLACK AND OTHER COLOURED PUG-DOGS

" (And then) I bought a dog—a queen !
  Ah, Tiny, dear, departing pug !
She lives, but she is past sixteen,
  And scarce can crawl across the rug.
I loved her, beautiful and kind ;
  Delighted in her pert Bow-wow :
But now she snaps if you don't mind ;
  'Twere lunacy to love her now.

I used to think, should e'er mishap
  Betide my crumpled-visaged Ti,
In shape of prowling thief, or trap,
  Or coarse bull-terrier—I should die.
But, ah ! disasters have their use ;
  And life might e'en be too sun-shiny :
Nor would I make myself a goose,
  If some big dog should swallow Tiny ! "
                    CALVERLEY : *Disasters.*

YOU will recollect the statement by Mr. Reginald F. Mayhew, given in the last chapter, that he had seen many pug-dogs born practically black in the old days and confined to the bucket on that account, and, also, the dog belonging to Queen Victoria in 1854.

Rawdon B. Lee, discussing the question as to whether black pug-dogs were produced in this country before the introduction from China by Lady Brassey, writes :

" Personally, I believe, there may be truth in both statements, that a black pug was accidentally produced and, at the same time, a specimen or two had been brought from the East."

But I have never heard of any pure black specimen being bred in this country prior to the Brassey introduction, though I have no doubt that had there been a demand for black specimens they could have been bred by carefully selective breeding of the darker fawn members, as there can be little doubt that many of the Russian and Chinese introductions had black ancestors.

There seems to be no doubt that Russia and, of course, China were breeding black specimens long before the blacks were known in this country.

W. D. Drury gives an account of the Brassey introduction. One of the dogs was called Mahdi, and Jack Spratt was the name of the other.

" It was in the autumn of 1886 that black Pugs were first brought into notice, a class being given for them at the Maidstone Show, all the exhibits being from the kennel of the late Lady Brassey. Two or three of these were compact, good-coated specimens, Jack Spratt, whose name appears as sire of all the early specimens, being the largest that was benched. Where Lady Brassey obtained her first specimen was never then clearly stated ; it was surmised that she became enamoured of a black Chinese Pug when she visited that country in the yacht the *Sunbeam*, and either purchased one, or mated a fawn female to a Chinese black dog. There is, however, some reason for thinking that black Pugs in England came from the fawns of King Duke's strain. Indeed, some breeders profess to have traced their history back to this dog. If they came from fawns, it seems just a little remarkable that they bred so true to colour as early as 1886."

I am given the date of the return of the *Sunbeam* to this country as 1884, and I have no doubt that this is approximately correct.

Frederick Gresham, writing in *Cassell's New Book of the Dog*, gives the names of the chief breeders and the best dogs after the introduction, to about 1909, but the present-day champions will be dealt with in the next chapter.

" The black Pug is a more recent production. He was brought into notice in 1886, when Lady Brassey exhibited some at the Maidstone Show. Mr. Rawdon Lee, however, tells us, in *Modern Dogs*, that the late Queen Victoria had one of the black variety in her possession half a century ago, and that a photograph of the dog is to be seen in one of the Royal albums. This, however, does not prove that a variety of black Pugs existed in any numbers. . . . The black Pug, however, came upon the scene about the time mentioned, and he came to stay. By whom he was manufactured is not a matter of much importance, as with the fawn Pug in existence there was not much difficulty in crossing it with the shortest-faced black dog of small size that could be found, and then back again to the fawn, and the thing was done. Fawn and black Pugs are continually being bred together, and, as a rule, if judgment is used in the selection of suitable crosses, the puppies are sound in colour, whether fawn or black. In every respect except markings the black Pug should be built on the same lines as the fawn, and be a cobby little dog with short back and well-developed hindquarters, wide in skull, with square and blunt muzzle and tightly curled tail. Her Majesty Queen Alexandra, when Princess of Wales, owned some very good black Pugs, but the first dog of the variety that could hold its own with the fawns was Ch. Duke Beira, a handsome fellow, who was the property of the late Miss C. F. A. Jenkinson. Then Mr. Summers startled the Pug world by buying the famous Ch. Chotee for £200. This price was, however, surpassed when the late Marquis of Anglesey gave £250 for Jack Valentine, who is still very much in evidence, sharing the hearthrug with his comrade Grindley King. Jack Valentine was bred by Miss J. W. Neish, who has a fine kennel of black Pugs at The Laws, in Forfarshire.

Dr. Tulk has a famous stud dog in Ch. Bobbie Burns, who is probably the shortest-faced black Pug that has ever been bred ; and a dog that has quickly forced his way to the front is Mrs. F. Howell's Ch. Mister Dandy, who is a beautiful specimen of the breed ; but the biggest winner up to the present time has been Miss Daniel's Ch. Bouji, an excellent specimen all round, who has proved himself an exceedingly good stud dog. Amongst other prominent exhibitors and breeders of black Pugs are Mrs. Raleigh Grey—who, in Rhoda, owned one of the best females of the breed—Miss H. Cooper, Mrs. Recketts and Mrs. Kingdon."

There is a rumour that is continually cropping up amongst the ignorant and the malicious that the black pug-dog was created by a cross between the fawn pug-dog and a black pomeranian. There are certainly some grounds for this statement, and the cross has often been effected, particularly in France, but the result is not a black pug-dog. In England it would be called a Heinz hound (forty different varieties), or a mongrel, but in France it has a name of its own—*Carlin à poil long*. These dogs resemble a black pug-dog, except that they have long silky coats and bushy tails which do not curl but are carried lightly over the back ; and as they were, no doubt, known in England prior to the introduction of the black pug-dog, they gave some grounds for the assumption that the black pug-dog was produced some-how through the breeding of short-coated from the long-coated varieties. The late Queen Alexandra had a dog of this description, of whom she was very fond, called Quiz. Flatterers called it an Alicante, but there seems little doubt that it was a freak or a mongrel *Carlin à poil long*.

Rawdon B. Lee mentions a dog of this type :

" Mrs. W. H. B. Warner, of Northallerton, at the close of 1893, showed a little black dog which she had brought from Japan, where it was said to be of a rare and choice breed. This is nothing else than a long-coated Pug—*i.e.* pug in character and shape, but with a jacket such as is seen on a Pomeranian."

In opposition to this I find W. D. Drury mentioning long-coated pug-dogs which he, apparently, believed to have been formed without the pomeranian cross.

"Rough-coated or long-haired Pugs are not very numerous, but they have appeared most frequently in the kennels owned by Mrs. Tulk and Miss Garniss. Only at intervals do they appear, and they always come from the strain owning Moss and Lamb as ancestors. These two dogs were said to have been 'captured' at Pekin well on to fifty years ago, and it is considered possible they may have had in their veins the blood of a long-coated Chinese dog. Mrs. Tulk has been successful in also breeding a long-coated black Pug."

In an interesting article upon pug-dogs, published in a paper on the 15th March 1902 under the signature of "La Vedette," the black pug-dog is described:

"As a faithful, intelligent and sympathetic companion, a dog who can be merry and light of heart and feet, or quiet and gentle, according to your mood of the moment, no better recommendation could be made than that of the subject of these lines."

The same article, writing of the fawns in comparison with the blacks, continues:

"Besides being placid of temper they are usually excellent trenchermen, and perhaps a little given—for the pug is a dog quite clever enough to know wherein lie his strength and influence—to trading upon the supposed delicacy of lung and bronchial tubes which characterise the race, and thereby, by the apt and timely expedient of a hollow cough or a snuffle, avoiding the dull but necessary walk in the rain, and ensuring a continuance of the snooze by the fire.

"But in the case of the black brother all this is changed. There can be no doubt whatever that black and fawn pugs are of exactly the same race. . . . At the same time, the black pug, unlike his human parallel, is a dog of far more lively and dominant personality than his pale brother. Black pugs have not that dislike to bad weather which occasionally confirms the fawns in evil courses, leading them to regard going out-of-doors in winter as more or less a penance ; they are untiringly active dogs."

So far as I can trace, no white pug-dog has ever been produced, despite the statement by W. D. Drury that :

"White Pugs did not win any friends when a few of them were benched some years back. . . . We never see any exhibited now, or hear of them being bred."

I think we can take it that none had been seen up to the days of Idstone, 1872, who mentions that he had inquired of many breeders, but could hear of no white specimen ever having been known. Since the date of Idstone, however, two dogs described as " white " pug-dogs have been exhibited in New York, and Miss Dalziel exhibited one at Birmingham in 1892. Both Rawdon B. Lee and Frederick Gresham, however, state that none of these dogs were white but only very light cream-fawns.

The only other coloured pug-dog is Miss Bellamy's strain of blue pug-dogs, of which there is a beautifully stuffed specimen in the British Museum (Natural History section). This strain came to be formed in rather a peculiar way. Miss Little crossed a fawn bitch with a black dog, and in the litter were two cream puppies with chocolate markings, a pure chocolate, and, in another litter, a brown. A black son of this sire was the sire of the " Bellamy Blues." These blue pug-dogs are rare and have never been popular.

CHAPTER VIII

THE TWENTIETH-CENTURY PUG-DOG

" The Pug (a diminutive and particularly ugly relative of the mastiff)."

J. R. AINSWORTH DAVIS, *The Natural History of Animals*, 1904.

I DO not intend to deal in this chapter with the respective merits of the various strains of pug-dogs exhibited at the present day, and I shall merely set out a schedule at the end of this book giving a list of the post-war champions and their owners. The best pre-war show dogs have been mentioned, and to go into the characters of the present-day specimens at any length would be out of keeping with the nature of this book, the intention of which is to give a short history of the breed during the 2600 years or so of its known existence. Further research by students into the earlier history of China will no doubt enable us to carry our history to an earlier date.

There can be no doubt that the pug-dog is increasing in numbers and popularity all over this country, and I trust that it will not be long before it regains the place to which it has always been entitled at the head of the list of toy-dogs.

To deal, however, with the history of the pug-dog in this century. At the beginning of the twentieth century the pug-dog was not popular. The pekinese was easily first favourite, and was followed by the pomeranian and toy-spaniels running fairly close together. The pug-dog took a rather poor fourth place.

The breed was subject to the usual attacks on the fallen from high estate, and it suffered from being a victim of the ancient and dishonourable sport of "kicking a dog when it's down."

Edwin Noble in his *Dog Lover's Book*, published in 1910, proved himself no pug-dog lover. The following are extracts from his book :

" Occasionally one sees a motor-car dashing through the London streets, and inside, seated beside the owner, will be a little dog wearing a pair of motor goggles, a little motor coat, a bell hanging from his blue collar, of course, and in wet, cold weather even a pair of warm gloves or shoes upon his forefeet. You cannot see very much of the dog himself, but you have no need to look twice to see that it is a Pug-dog—for no other dog would submit to being made such a ' Guy.' . . .

" The best stories which stand to the Pug's credit are one in which, after an absence of two and a half years, he recognises the maid who used to wash him, and another in which a Pug-dog used to carry a collecting-box upon his back to collect funds to provide luxuries for our troops during the South African War ; when he met anybody he would deliberately stop and shake his box to attract their attention."

But Mr. Noble hastens to add, and at length, that any other breed could have done the same things, only very much better !

I take the first extract from Mr. Noble's book to be a compliment in showing the placidity of the pug-dog in submitting to the wishes of his owners even if they are unpleasant. But, as a matter of fact, I believe Mr. Noble has mistaken the breed, as I have never heard of a pug-dog " guyed " in the fashion he mentions, though the French bulldog certainly suffered from this form of imbecility in its owners. I do not deny that pug-dogs at the beginning of this century often had bells on their collars like other toys.

But there were other writers willing to give the pug-dog his due, and C. H. Lane, in his *All about Dogs*, published in 1900, describes him as follows :

" One of the really old-fashioned pets and companions is the Pug, of which I have for the last thirty years generally had some specimen in my house, and usually, when I have judged the breed, have been favoured with record entries. I remember on one occasion, when I had a very heavy day at an important London show, and had taken an immense amount of trouble, in the open, on a broiling day in June or July, when the whole of my exhibitors were of the fair sex, and ranged from the highest in the Kennel-world, Her Royal Highness, the Princess of Wales, to those who would not be ashamed to be included amongst ' the working classes.'

" A very smart, showy and active dog, often *an arrant coward*, but with a great appearance of dignity, and even ferocity, which is not without its impression on the public. My experience of the breed is that they are, as a rule, very affectionate, and devoted to their owners, ' good-doers ' and nearly always ready for anything in the way of eating and drinking, great lovers of comfort, and very jealous of any other members of the doggy community being made as much of as themselves. They are very lively, bustling companions, and very popular with those who have kept them."

F. T. Barton, too, wrote at length on the pug-dog in his *Our Dogs and All about Them*, from which I have extracted the following :

" This is a very old variety of Toy-dog, and one that always maintains its popularity, though, to a considerable extent, it has been displaced by such breeds as the Pomeranian, the Pekinese, etc., etc. ; yet, in spite of this, as a dog for companionship for children, it has certainly no superior, even if it has any equal.

" Successive generations of such associateship have

conferred upon it that degree of docility so essential for such purposes.

"No amount of provocation seems to disturb the temperament of the Pug, yet, in spite of this, it can be obstinate to a degree, such obstinacy usually revealing itself during the forcible administration of medicine, etc., etc. . . .

"The Pug was introduced into Great Britain from China. . . .

"At one time attempts were made to breed white Pugs, but the experiments were not carried far enough. . . . As a breed the Pug is hardy."

The forbearance of the pug-dog with children, which Mr. Barton mentions, was very early recognised, and there is rather a gruesome description of a case of this in Lieut.-Col. Charles Hamilton Smith's *Mammalia*, in "The Naturalist's Library," which was published in 1840 :

"We have witnessed forbearance in one " (pug-dog) " belonging to a lady, whose child bit the dog until he yelled, but never showed anger, or a disposition to get away."

I would like just to mention the names of two people who have been great pug-dog lovers during this century, and both of whom have passed away. Both bred and kept pug-dogs, and both did the breed the greatest possible good in their different stations of life. The first is the late Queen Alexandra and the second is my old friend, the late Mr. Courtney Thorpe.

I can only find one trace of the breed being kept by the present Royal family. This was in an article appearing in *The Ludgate*, for October 1897. In this article it is stated that the then Duchess of York (now H.M. the Queen) had a burial-ground for her pet dogs at Oaklands Park in Surrey. The article is illustrated by a photograph of various canine tombstones, on one of which

I can decipher the following words : " Topsy a pug and Dinah her . . . mother."

Having dealt with some owners I will mention one pug-dog. The following extract is taken from a cutting from *Lloyd's Newspaper* in 1905 :

" A pug that lives in Richmond has been taught to let the cat climb on his back and to carry her round the room to dinner. They both dine. off the same plate. When the meal is finished the mistress says to the Pug, ' Now, Sam, make Toushan pay for her dinner.' Sam then growls, and strikes puss on the face with his paw, a familiarity which the cat resents by boxing the dog's ears."

In the north of England, and in Scotland in particular, an increase in the popularity of the breed has been shown during the past few years, and it was found necessary for a new club to be created. This was The Scottish Pug-Dog Club, of which the first president was Miss Hatrick and the first hon. secretary was Miss M'Kay. The club was founded in 1925. The present president and hon. secretary are, respectively, Mr. R. E. M'Nair and Mrs. M'Craw of 38 West Bowling Green Street, Leith.

Pug-dogs of this country are now being bred slightly smaller than their Victorian brothers, and the breed is living up to the title it was given long ago of being " the grand little breed," and it is fulfilling the motto given it by the Pug-Dog Club of " Multum in parvo."

I am very glad to be able to say that all over the country the sterling worth of the " grand little breed " is being realised. The fact of its great gift of perfect health and the very little trouble needed to keep it always in perfect condition, is at last being accepted, and gives it a great pull over the long-coated breeds of toy dogs. I would like to end with that one particular quality which has been noted from the very earliest days. In the words of W. D. Drury :

" One quality they possess above most breeds, which is a strong recommendation for them as lap-dog, and that is their cleanliness, and freedom from any offensive smell of breath or skin."

CHAPTER IX

THE PUG-DOG IN AMERICA

"After the close of the Napoleonic Wars he" (the pug-dog), "found his way across the Channel to England. . . ."
CAPTAIN A. H. TRAPMAN : *The Dog : Man's Best Friend.* 1929.[1]

THE fashions in dogs in the United States of America seem to fluctuate in very much the same way as they do in this country, but to a less marked extent, though the favourite breed appears always to be the same in the two countries.

The popularity of the pug-dog here in about 1880 was echoed slightly later in the U.S.A., by a large increase in its pug-dog population. And, again, the advent of the pekinese here was felt in the U.S.A. towards the beginning of this century. To-day, both in the U.S.A. and here, by far the most popular toy-dog is the pekinese.

Before the European discovery of America, three breeds of dog are said to have been known in South America. "The largest of these was an animal of medium size, with slender head and legs. . . . The second was a short-legged dog, somewhat resembling a dachshund, which, to judge from a vase-painting, was also used in the class. The third was a kind of pug, probably kept as a lap-dog." [2] But apart from these

[1] Should Mr. Trapman desire a pseudonym for the second edition of his book, might I suggest, "The Man : Pug's Worst Friend ! "
[2] Joyce, *South American Archaeology.*

natives it seems difficult to trace the arrival of the first Christopher Columbus pug-dog. Specimens, no doubt, crossed over with the settlers in the early eighteenth century during the time of the popularity of the breed in this country. They were clearly known at the time of Washington Irving (1783–1859).

When dog-shows began in the U.S.A., the breed was taken up by Dr. Cryer, and the history of American pugdom may be said to have really started with this gentleman.

Dr. Cryer was the author of a book written exclusively on pug-dogs, and he did a tremendous amount of good for pug-dog breeding in the U.S.A. Nearly all the early show specimens were imported from this country, and, as we will see, were nearly all of the Mayhew strain.

I do not think I can do better than to quote at length from James Watson, who wrote from the U.S.A., and gives the American point of view :

" The usefulness of the Click blood seems to have been in the production of successful dams, for outside of Odin and Toby, the sire of Dr. Cryer's Dolly, it is hardly possible to trace back to Click in the male line. On the other hand we find, in that very hard-to-get and useful book Dr. Cryer published in 1891, *Prize Pugs*, his extensions of pedigrees of the leading winning dogs of America up to that time show that fifty per cent. of them, and those including nearly all the best dogs, had this Click cross. Bob Ivy, Dr. Cryer's best production, had three crosses, being inbred to Dolly on the sire's side, and Dolly was by Toby, and on the dam's side going back to Vic, by Click out of Leech's or Lock's Judy. This Vic was also the dam of Tum Tum II., a remarkably good dog by Max. Imported Othello also traces to Vic. From the Click-Gipsey cross we find Judy, dam to Tragedy, and from the Click-Topsy came Cloudy, who was dam of Comedy, also of Dowager the dam of Queen Rose and Duchess of Connaught. Queen Rose was dam of Champion Loris. Cloudy was also dam

6

of Lady Flora, whose daughter, Lady Cloudy, was the
dam of Kash, a prominent winner here in 1889 and
1890.

" There was quite a run on the get of the dog Toby
on the part of American exhibitors after Dr. Cryer's
Dolly had made her mark, and Lord Nelson and Miss
Whitney's Young Toby were by him. Toby was by
Click out of Mrs. Mayhew's Hebe, by Crusoe out of
Phyllis, a part Willoughby bitch. Notwithstanding we
had some close-up descendants of this inbred Pekin
strain of pug, not one of the entire number that were
exhibited showed any indication of the build of Lamb and
Moss, the long and low type which Mr. Mayhew says
they were, and which we see in most of the long-haired
Pekinese which have come direct from China to England
or here. Dr. Ivy, father of the then little boy after
whom Dr. Cryer named his best production, very
kindly sent us from Shanghai photographs of what the
owner named Pekin Pugs, and Dr. Ivy said the dog
was a high-class specimen. This we submitted to Mr.
Mayhew to see how the dog might conform to his re-
collection of Lamb and Moss, and he replied as follows :
' There is no more resemblance to Lamb or Moss than
to any pug of the present day. Neither Lamb, Moss nor
Click had a white hair, nor had any of the latter's
progeny. The dog is apparently a smooth Pekinese,
just as there are smooth-coated specimens in the rough-
coated varieties of terriers. Lamb, Moss and Click
were as profuse coated as are the descendants of a certain
line of smooth fox terriers. A very large proportion of
Click's sons and daughters, however, had the orthodox
length of coat, nor was it transmitted in subsequent
generations.'

" The first pug of quality shown in this country was
Dr. Cryer's Roderick, a dog of nice size, handicapped
by very straight hind legs to the extent of being double
jointed. It was this defect that enabled Mrs. Pue's
larger dog George to defeat him in the majority of cases
when they met. Both of these dogs were inferior to little
Banjo, which was one of the kennel of dogs brought over
in 1881 by Mr. Mason, but which unfortunately was

smothered while in transit to London, Ont., show that fall. He was the sire of Lovat, one of the very best show dogs and sires of his day in England. Of the bitches of that time the best by a good margin was Mr. Knight's Effie, which won in the open class at New York in 1882, beating Dr. Cryer's Dolly. Effie afterwards won three championships at New York, but unfortunately she was a non-breeder. The next good pug was the dog which was here known as Joe, but whose proper name was Zulu II., the change of name being the result of an error on the part of the young man sent over from England in charge of Miss Lee's dogs. The real Joe was sold as Zulu II. before the dogs went to Pittsburgh show, and Zulu II. was shown as Joe and got second to Sambo. Dr. Cryer wanted to buy ' Joe ' and offered the catalogue price of fifteen pounds to the secretary of the show, who declined it, saying that he had bought the dog. The fact is that the young man had found out his mistake and got the officials to protect him. Coming back to New York the young man got short of funds, and left the dog to pay his board bill ; the owner then went to Mr. Mortimer, who recognised the dog and bought him, and at the New York show of a few weeks later, Joe appeared in his new owner's name, and won. There was quite a little talk about the seeming peculiarity of these proceedings, but it was all cleared up and the *bona fides* of Mr. Mortimer's purchase thoroughly established. Joe, as he continued to be called, was by Comedy out of a pedigreeless bitch, and he continued his successful career till 1887, winning altogether twelve championships, most of them for Mr. George H. Hill, of Madeira, O. He was also the sire of a number of good pugs.

"After Joe the next good dog imported was Bradford Ruby, a son of Lovat. An excellent pug, just a trifle large, and slightly leggy. This dog had won many prizes before being imported, but when he made his first appearance here at the New York show, the late Hugh Dalziel, who ought to have not only known what a good pug was, but also known what this pug was, gave Bradford Ruby a v.h.r. card. There were sixteen dogs in the open class, which shows how popular pugs were at that time, but all the good dogs were in the v.h.r. division, and the three placed animals were plain, ordinary specimens, not one of which distinguished himself after that.   As it was now necessary to win three firsts in open class, Bradford Ruby's record in the latter class is not so good as that of Joe, but he won nine firsts in the champion class. After Ruby came Master Tragedy, Othello and Lord Clover, none of them in the class of Ruby. Othello was really the best of the three, but he was rather large and his colour smutty. Master Tragedy fell far short of what we expected on his English reputation.

"The home-bred pugs of Dr. Cryer now became the prominent feature in the breed, beginning with his Max and Bessie, both out of imported Dolly, who was by the Click dog Toby. Then came Dude, also out of Dolly, but he was sold, and finally Dude's son Bob Ivy. 'Little Bob' was a fitting culmination to the doctor's breeding, for business now compelled him to gradually give up the fascinations of improving and showing pugs. Bob Ivy was a very nice little dog in every way, and his size was all one could desire. Bessie used to beat him for the specials for best in the show, but after the little dog had matured he was hard to beat. In front of him at New York in 1890 was a very smart young imported dog, Tim, by the English dog Max, but he died the same year.

"As the pedigree of Bob Ivy covers the ground very fully for most of the pedigree of dogs of that time, we give it in full [at top of page opposite].

"Pugs went on the down grade after 1890, and with the arrival of new attractions in the way of toy-dogs, such as Pomeranians, and the pushing of Japanese and English spaniels to the front, they became fewer by degrees and beautifully less, until we have now to rely almost entirely upon one exhibitor, the well-known Al. Eberhardt, of Camp Dennison, O. It looked at one time as if there might be a turn for the better, that being when Mrs. Howard Gould was showing a few black pugs, but they did not catch on as they should

" Bob Ivy

Bred and owned by Dr. M. H. Cryer ; born April 23, 1888

Pedigree.

```
Sire:        ┌ Ch. Max        ┌ Ch. Roderick ┌ Ch. Punch (E. 6761)
Ch.          │                │              │   By Lord Willoughby's
Dude         │                │              │     Jumbo.
             │                └ Imp. Dolly  . Morris' Judy.
             │                              ┌ Click ┌ Lamb, from Pekin.
             │                ┌ Toby ┤      │       └ Moss, from Pekin.
             │                │      │      └ Crusoe.
             └ Imp. Dolly ┤   │      └ Hebe ┤          ┌ Tomahawk.
                          │   │             └ Phyllis ┤              ┌ Jumbo.
                          │   │                       └ Fatima II. └ Fatima.
                          └ Liz. ┌ Ch. Punch
                                 └ Molly, by Ch. Baron ┌ Cupid.
                                                       └ Ruby.
```

```
Dam:        ┌ Imp. Othello ┌ Othello ┌ Skylark        ┌ Guss.
Vesta       │              │         │                └ Eden.
            │              │         └ Judy
            │              │                  ┌ Tum Tum II. . Max ┌ Sam.
            │              └ Scamp II. ┤      │                   └ Rose.
            │                         │      │                         ┌ Click ┌ Lamb.
            │                         └ Belle Petite . Vic ┤           │       └ Moss.
            │                                              │ Leech's   └
            └ Imp. (Pedigree unknown).                     └ Judy.
```

have, and it is Eberhardt's pugs or a blank at nearly all the shows for the past year or two.

" There is no reason why this breed should be neglected in this way. Compare the pug with any of the popular fancies and it will stand the test. Tastes differ, but to our mind the character and beauty of wrinkle in the head of such a dog as Ding Dong is far ahead of the abnormally developed Japanese spaniel, for instance. Look at the care called for by these long-coated dogs, and the impossibility of making a pet and companion of any of the long, silky-coated toys. The pug needs no more coddling than a hardy terrier, nor any more care in coat. He is a dog that has always had a reputation for keeping himself clean and tidy, and they used to say that he had less doggy perfume than any other house dog. He may not be quite so demonstrative as some of the effervescing little toys, but he is just as intelligent and has a dignity and composure all his own.

" Ere long we fully expect to see the black pugs become popular, for they are certainly very attractive in their brilliant coat of black satin. As Mr. Mayhew says, they are apt to be 'tight-skinned' and fail to show the wrinkle such as Ding Dong displays; but a few do show improvement in that direction, and it is only a matter of careful selection and breeding such as one has to carry out in all breeds to reach success. There is a good field here for those who want to take up something that is bound eventually to become a popular breed."

From the day of which Mr. Watson writes to the present, there has not been a revival of the breed in the U.S.A., and the beauties of the black have not been appreciated there. This is a joy for them which is yet to come. Registrations at the American Kennel Club were fifteen in 1926 and only three for the months January to November inclusive during 1927, against the 283 registered in England in 1927. But it is interesting to note that for the year 1926, apart from the pekinese which scored 229 registrations against 3627 in England (1927), and the pomeranian which scored 96 against our 1412 (1927), the pug-dog secured more registrations than any other toy-dog in the U.S.A.

The demand from the U.S.A. for the exportation of good pug-dogs from this country has, however, of recent years, been slowly but surely increasing. Mrs. Power, of Birmingham, has sent across some good dogs during the last few years.

I, too, have sent recently two fawn bitch puppies to purchasers in Canada, and it has been my experience, which I have no doubt other breeders will endorse, that, with regard to pug-dogs, once planted in a new country or district they quickly bear fruit. He is seen, hardly believed and an immediate demand comes for further specimens.

SCHEDULE OF SHOW POINTS

I HAVE set out below the standard of show points drawn up by Stonehenge and published in his *Dogs of the British Islands*, in 1878, which preceded by over five years the first list of show points issued by the Pug-Dog Club. Below it I have given the latest standard of points issued by the Pug-Dog Club.

A few words, however, are necessary before the Stonehenge points can be clearly understood.

It was a common practice of breeders of bull-dogs to cross their dogs with pug-dogs, and most of the winning bull-dogs in the early show days had the pug-dog cross. This was naturally opposed by the breeders of pug-dogs, and pug-dogs with a trace of the bull-dog in them were regarded with the greatest disfavour.

This practice started in very early days, George Edwards (1694–1773) mentioning in his chapter on "Bull-dogs" that "Dutch mastiffs or pug-dogs" were used "by accident or design" to "improve the bull-dogs." Stonehenge also mentions the practice in his day, and Frederick Gresham, in *Cassell's New Book of the Dog*, writes that :

" It is known that it " (the pug-dog) "has been bred with the Bull-dog for the anticipated benefit of the latter."

It is with this in mind that we must consider the standard issued in 1878 by Stonehenge.

POINTS OF THE MODERN PUG

	Value.		Value.		Value.
Head	10	Trace	5	Legs and feet	10
Ears	5	Colour	10	Tail	10
Eyes	5	Coat	10	Symmetry and size	5
Moles	5	Neck	5		
Mask, vent and wrinkles.	10	Body	10		
	35		40		25

GRAND TOTAL . 100

1. The *head* (value 10) should have a round, monkey-like skull, and should be of considerable girth, but in proportion not so great as that of the bull-dog. The face is short, but, again, not " bully " or retreating, the end being cut off square ; and the teeth must be level —if undershot, a cross of the bull is almost always to be relied on. Tongue large, and often hanging out of the mouth ; but this point is not to be accepted for or against the individual. The cheek is very full and muscular.

2. The *ears* (value 5) are small, vine-shaped and thin, and should lie moderately flat on the face (formerly they were invariably closely cropped, but this practice is now quite out of fashion) ; they are black, with a slight mixture of fawn hair.

3. The *eyes* (value 5) are dark brown and full, with a soft expression. There should be no tendency to weep, as in the toy spaniel.

4. A *black mole* (value 5) is always demanded on each cheek, with two or three hairs springing from it ; the regulation number of these is three, but of course it is easy to reduce them to that number.

5. *Mask, vent and wrinkles* (value 10).—These markings must be taken together, as they all depend mainly on colour. The wrinkles, it is true, are partly in the skin ; but over and above these there should be lines of black, corresponding with them, on the face and

forehead. The mask should extend over the whole face as jet black, reaching a little above the eyes, and the vent should be of the same colour. In the Willoughby strain the black generally extends higher up the skull, and has not the same definite edge as in the Morrison pug, in which this point is well shown and greatly insisted on by its admirers.

6. A *trace* (value 5) or black line is exhibited along the top of the back by all perfect pugs ; and the clearer this is, the better. As with the mask, so with this—the definition is more clear in the Morrison than in the Willoughby pug. When it extends widely over the back it is called a " saddle mark," and this is often displayed in the Willoughby, though seldom met with in the Morrison strain ; of course, it is admired in the one, and deprecated in the other, by their several supporters.

7. The *colour* (value 10) of the Morrison pug is a rich yellow-fawn, while that of the Willoughby is a cold stone. The salmon-fawn is never met with in good specimens of either, and is objected to. In the Willoughby the fawn-coloured hairs are apt to be tipped with black, but in its rival the fawn colour is pure, and unmixed with any darker shade. Of course, in inbred specimens the colour is often intermediate.

8. The *coat* (value 10) is short, soft and glossy over the whole body, but on the tail it is longer and rougher. A fine tail indicates a bull cross.

9. The *neck* (value 5) is full, stout and muscular, but without any tendency to dewlap ; which again indicates, when present, that the bull-dog cross has been resorted to.

10. The *body* (value 10) is very thick and strong, with a wide chest and round ribs ; the loin should be very muscular, as well as the quarters, giving a general punchy look, almost peculiar to this dog.

11. *Legs and feet* (value 10).—The legs should be straight but fine in bone, and should be well clothed with muscle. As to the feet, they must be small, and in any case narrow. In both strains the toes are well split up ; but in the Willoughby the shape of the foot is cat-like, while the Morrison strain has a hare foot. There should be no white on the toes, and the nails should be dark.

12. The *tail* (value 10) must curve so that it lies flat on the side, not rising above the back to such an extent as to show daylight through it. The curl should extend to a little more than one circle.

13. *Size and symmetry* (value 5).—In size the pug should be from 10 to 12 inches high—the smaller the better. A good specimen should be very symmetrical.

. . . .

I present the points now in force and drawn up by the Pug-Dog Club, without comment :

REVISED STANDARD OF POINTS OF THE PUG-DOG CLUB

				FAWN. Points.	BLACK. Points.
Symmetry	.	.	.	10	10
Size	.	.	.	5	10
Condition .	.	.	.	5	5
Body	.	.	.	10	10
Legs Feet	.	.	.	5	5
Head	.	.	.	5	5
Muzzle	.	.	.	10	10
Ears	.	.	.	5	5
Eyes	.	.	.	10	10
Mask	.	.	.	5	—
Wrinkles	.	.	.	5	5
Tail	.	.	.	10	10
Trace	.	.	.	5	—
Coat	.	.	.	5	5
Colour	.	.	.	5	10

ACKNOWLEDGED POINTS

Symmetry.—Symmetry and general appearance, decidedly square and cobby. A lean, leggy Pug and a dog with short legs and a long body are equally objectionable.

Size and Condition.—The Pug should be *multum in parvo*, but this condensation (if the word may be used) should be shown by compactness of form, well-knit proportions, and hardness of developed muscle. Weight, from 14 to 18 lb. (dog or bitch) desirable.

Body.—Short and cobby, wide in chest and well ribbed up.

Legs.—Very strong, straight, of moderate length, and well under.

Feet.—Neither so long as the foot of the hare, nor so round as that of the cat ; well-split-up toes, and the nails black.

Muzzle.—Short, blunt, square, but not upfaced.

Head.—Large, massive, round—not apple-headed, with no indentation of the skull.

Eyes.—Dark in colour, very large, bold and prominent, globular in shape, soft and solicitous in expression, very lustrous, and, when excited, full of fire.

Ear.—Thin, small, soft, like black velvet. There are two kinds—the " Rose " and "Button." Preference is given to the latter.

Markings.—Clearly defined. The muzzle or mask, ears, moles on cheeks, thumb-mark or diamond on forehead, black-trace should be as black as possible.

Mask.—The mask should be black. The more intense and well-defined, the better.

Wrinkles.—Large and deep.

Trace.—A black line extending from the occiput to the tail.

Tail.—Curled tightly as possible over the hip. The double curl is perfection.

Coat.—Fine, smooth, soft, short and glossy, neither hard nor woolly.

Colour.—Silver or apricot-fawn. Each should be decided, to make the contrast complete between the colour and the trace and the mask.

.   .   .   .

There is no need to set out in full the show points issued by the Scottish Pug-Dog Club in 1925, as they are very similar to those of the Pug-Dog Club.

The " acknowledged points " are almost word for word the same, with the exception of the weight, which is given by the Scottish Club as "from 13 to 17 lb. (Dog or Bitch)."

The " standard of points " varies very slightly. Both blacks and fawns are given 10 points for legs and feet, whilst the tail is only given 5.

SCHEDULE OF POST-WAR CHAMPIONS

LIST OF PUG-DOGS ATTAINING CHAMPIONSHIP STATUS BETWEEN 1918 AND 1st JANUARY 1930

Name of Owner at Time of Championship.	Name of Dog.	Sex.	Date.
Mrs. V. Curtis . .	Ch. Penelope	B.	7/6/21
Mrs. C. Demaine .	Ch. Dark Ducas	D.	15/3/21
,, ,, .	Ch. Dark Dickory	D.	13/2/24
,, ,, .	Ch. Dark Dragoon	D.	4/5/27
Mrs. M. C. Gibbon .	Ch. Tinker Bell	B.	12/4/28
Mrs. C. Harriott .	Ch. Master Teddie	D.	2/2/21
Miss M. D. Hatrick .	Ch. Master Pen of Inver	D.	13/7/26
,, ,, .	Ch. Penella of Inver	B.	12/12/28
Misses M. D. Hatrick, R. M. Morrison and A. M. Campbell	Ch. Miss Penelope	B.	8/10/24
Miss E. E. Higham .	Ch. Rachel of Noyon	B.	10/2/26
Mrs. H. C. Lake .	Ch. Narcissus of Otter	D.	11/2/25
,, ,, .	Ch. Dancing Dickerine of Otter	B.	3/5/28
Mr. G. W. Lawrie .	Ch. Springbird	D.	13/12/22
Mrs. P. Lindley .	Ch. Felix of Otter	D.	3/5/28
Miss C. R. Little .	Ch. Caro-li of Baronshalt	B.	13/7/26
Miss A. W. Low .	Ch. Turret Meshach	D.	3/11/20
Mrs. M. Micklem .	Ch. Prowett Pretty Polly	B.	28/9/27
Mrs. E. M. Power .	Ch. Lord Tom Noddy of Broadway	D.	16/2/21
,, ,, .	Ch. Prowett Pansy	B.	12/5/21

Name of Owner at Time of Championship.	Name of Dog.	Sex.	Date.
Mrs. E. M. Power .	Ch. Bogey Man of Broadway	D.	4/7/23
,, ,, .	Ch. Allermuir Dolly	B.	1/10/24
,, ,, .	Ch. Rajah of Broadway	D.	25/3/25
,, ,, .	Ch. Veronica of Broadway	B.	1/9/26
,, ,, .	Ch. Scaramouche of Broadway	D.	23/3/27
,, ,, .	Ch. Bo-Peep of Broadway	B.	23/3/27
,, ,, .	Ch. Field Marshal of Broadway	D.	7/12/27
Mrs. Prowett Ferdinands	Ch. Young Scotland	D.	16/6/20
,, ,,	Ch. Prowett Perfection	B.	20/10/20
,, ,,	Ch. Jane of Otter	B.	14/11/23
Miss E. M. Seed .	Ch. Prowett Prudence	B.	4/10/22
Miss A. Spurling .	Ch. Hiawatha	D.	1/9/26
Miss C. M. Topp .	Ch. Dark Scotsman	D.	4/9/29
Miss H. A. Voy . .	Ch. Paul of Inver	D.	20/3/29
Mrs. R. Watt . .	Ch. Jolly Onyx	D.	5/9/23
Mrs. H. Welford . .	Ch. Off Side	B.	6/7/20
Miss M. Wooldridge	Ch. Towcester Touchwood	D.	3/11/20
Lord Wrottesley .	Ch. Princess Pretty	B.	5/4/23
,, ,, .	Ch. Dapper Dandy	D.	27/10/27
,, ,, .	Ch. Dainty Duchess	B.	7/12/27
,, ,, .	Ch. Angelico	D.	3/10/28

Lightning Source UK Ltd.
Milton Keynes UK
UKOW052110291111

182866UK00001B/77/A